Learn Swedish In 7 DAYS!

The Ultimate Crash Course to Learning the Basics of the Swedish Language in No Time

By Dagny Taggart

Disclaimer

The information provided in this book is designed to provide helpful information on the subjects discussed. The author's books are only meant to provide the reader with the basics knowledge of a certain language, without any warranties regarding whether the student will, or will not, be able to incorporate and apply all the information provided. Although the writer will make her best effort share her insights, language learning is a difficult task, and each person needs a different timeframe to fully incorporate a new language. This book, nor any of the author's books constitute a promise that the reader will learn a certain language within a certain timeframe.

Table of Contents

Dedicated to those who love going beyond their own frontiers.

Keep on traveling,

Dagny Taggart

My FREE Gift to You!

As a way of saying thank you for downloading my book, I'd like to send you an exclusive gift that will revolutionize the way you learn new languages. It's an extremely comprehensive PDF with 15 language hacking rules that **will help you learn 300% <u>faster</u>, with <u>less effort</u>, and with <u>higher than ever retention rates</u>**.

This guide is an amazing complement to the book you just got, and could easily be a stand-alone product, but for now I've decided to give it away for free, to thank you for being such an awesome reader, and to make sure I give you all the value that I can to help you succeed faster on your language learning journey.

To get your FREE gift, go to the link below, follow the steps, and I'll send it to your email address right away.

>> <u>http://bitly.com/Language-Gift</u> <<

GET **INSTANT** ACCESS

Learn Any Language 300% FASTER

>> Get Full Online Language Courses With Audio Lessons <<

Would you like to learn a new language? I think that's a great idea. Now, why don't you do it 300% *FASTER*?

I've partnered with the most revolutionary language teachers to bring you the very language online courses I've ever seen. It's a mind-blowing program specifically created for language hackers such as ourselves. It will allow you learn ANY language, from French to Chinese, 3x faster, straight from the comfort of your own home, office, or wherever you may be. It's like having an unfair advantage!

You can choose from a wide variety of languages, such as French, Spanish, Italian, German, Chinese, Portuguese, and A TON more.

Each Online Course consists of:

+ 91 Built-In Lessons
+ 33 Interactive Audio Lessons
+ 24/7 Support to Keep You Going

The program is extremely engaging, fun, and easy-going. You won't even notice you are learning a complex foreign language from scratch. And before you realize it, by the time you go through all the lessons you will officially become a truly solid speaker.

Old classrooms are a thing of the past. It's time for a revolution.

If you'd like to go the extra mile, the click the button below or follow the link, and let the revolution begin

>> http://www.bitly.com/Foreign-Languages <<

Introduction

Most people are daunted by the idea of learning a language. They think it's impossible, even unfathomable. I remember as a junior in high school, watching footage of Jackie O giving a speech in French. I was so impressed and inspired by the ease at which she spoke this other language of which I could not understand one single word.

At that moment, I knew I had to learn at least one foreign language. I started with Spanish, later took on Mandarin, and most recently have started learning Portuguese. No matter how challenging and unattainable it may seem, millions of people have done it. You do NOT have to be a genius to learn another language. You DO have to be willing to take risks and make mistakes, sometimes even make a fool of yourself, be dedicated, and of course, practice, practice, practice!

This book will only provide you with the basics in order to get started learning the Swedish language. It is geared towards those who are planning to travel to Sweden and covers many common scenarios you may find yourself in so feel free to skip around to the topic that is most prudent to you at the moment. Learning Swedish will also make it easier to understand other Nordic languages, especially Norwegian, since they are rather similar.

In the Swedish language there are several English loanwords that you will recognize. In several cases the pronunciation is the same, but far from always. And Swedish also contain 3 original characters that doesn't exist in the English alphabet. Those are "å", "ä" and "ö" (Å, Ä and Ö).

I will now list some tips that I have found useful and should be very helpful to you in your journey of learning Swedish. I don't wish you luck because that will not get you anywhere- reading this book, dedicating yourself, and taking some risks will!

Tip #1 - Keep an Open Mind

It may seem obvious but you must understand that languages are very different from each other. You cannot expect them to translate word for word. Many foreigners coming to Sweden often speak "backwords" and use the wrong connective verbs. E.g. when trying to say that *"I am not happy"* they in Swedish say *"Jag inte vara glad"* instead of the correct *"Jag är inte glad"*. As you can see the sentence structure is much the same in Swedish and English which will make it easier for you. But there are of course major differences. As in English some words could mean several different things and there are differences depending on if you should be formal or informal, so keep your mind open to the many differences that you will find in the language that go far beyond just the words.

Tip #2 - Take Risks

Be fearless. Talk to as many people as you can. The more practice you get the better and don't worry about looking like a fool when you say, "*I am pregnant*" rather than "*I am embarrassed,*" which as you will find out can be a common mistake. If anyone is laughing remember they are not laughing at you. Just laugh with them, move on, and LEARN from it, which brings us to our next tip.

Tip #3 - Learn from your Mistakes

It doesn't help to get down because you made one more mistake when trying to order at a restaurant, take a taxi, or just in a friendly conversation. Making mistakes is a HUGE part of learning a language. You have to put yourself out there as we said and be willing to make tons of mistakes! Why? Because what can you do with mistakes. You can LEARN from them. If you never make a mistake, you probably are not learning as much as you could. So every time you mess up when trying to communicate, learn from it, move on, and keep your head up!

Tip #4 - Immerse yourself in the language

If you're not yet able to go to Sweden, try to pretend that you are. Surround yourself with Swedish. Listen to music in Swedish, watch movies and TV shows in Swedish. Play games on your phone, computer, etc. in Swedish. Another great idea is to actually put your phone, computer, tablet and/or other electronic devices in Swedish. It can be frustrating at first but in the end this exposure will definitely pay off.

Tip #5 - Start Thinking in Swedish

I remember being a senior in high school and working as a lifeguard at a fairly deserted pool. While I was sitting and staring at the empty waters, I would speak to myself or think to myself (to not seem so crazy) in Spanish. I would describe my surroundings, talk about what I had done and what I was going to do, etc. While I was riding my bike, I would do the same thing. You can do the same thing with Swedish. During any activity when you don't need to talk or think about anything else, keep your brain constantly going in Swedish to get even more practice in the language. So get ready to turn off the English and jumpstart your Swedish brain!

Tip #6 - Label your Surroundings/Use Flashcards

When I started to learn Portuguese, I bought an excellent book that included stickers so that you could label your surroundings. So I had stickers all over my parents' house from the kitchen to the bathroom that labeled the door, the dishes, furniture, parts of the house, etc. It was a great, constant reminder of how to say these objects in another language. You can just make your own labels and stick them all over the house and hope it doesn't bother your family or housemates too much!

Tip #7 - Use Context clues, visuals, gestures, expressions, etc.

If you don't understand a word that you have heard or read, look or listen to the surrounding words and the situation to help you. If you are in a restaurant and your friend says, "I am going to ??? a sandwich." You can take a guess that she said *order* or *eat* but you don't have to understand every word in order to understand the general meaning. When you are in a conversation use gestures, expressions, and things around you to help communicate your meaning. Teaching English as a second language to young learners taught me this. If you act everything out, you are more likely to get your point across. If you need to say the word *bird* and you don't know how you can start flapping your arms and chirping and then you will get your point across and possibly learn how to say *bird*. It may seem ridiculous but as

I said, you have to be willing to look silly to learn another language and this greatly helps your language communication and learning.

Tip #8 - Circumlocution

Circumlo... what? This is just a fancy word for describing something when you don't know how to say it. If you are looking to buy an umbrella and don't know how to say it, what can you do? You can describe it using words you know. You can say, it is something used for the rain that opens and closes and then hopefully someone will understand you, help you, and maybe teach you how to say this word. Using circumlocution is excellent language practice and is much better than just giving up when you don't know how to say a word. So keep talking even if you have a limited vocabulary. Say what you can and describe or act out what you can't!

SECTION 1: THE BASICS

Chapter 1
Getting the Pronunciation Down

Below I will break down general Swedish pronunciation for the whole alphabet dividing it into vowels and consonants. One great thing about Swedish is that the letters almost always stay consistent as far as what sound they make, especially the vowels. Unlike English in which the vowels can make up to 27 different sounds depending on how they are mixed. Be thankful that you don't have to learn English or at least have already learned English. There are of course some sounds in Spanish that we never make in English and you possibly have never made in your life. Apart from the unique vowels "å", "ä" and "ö" some consonants are pronounced different depending how they are combined. So get ready to start moving your mouth and tongue in a new way that may seem strange at first but as I keep saying, practice makes perfect!

The charts on the next page will explain how to say the letter, pronounce it, and if there is an example in an English word of how to say it I put it in the right column.

Vowel Sounds

Vowel	How to say the letter	How to pronounce it in a word	As in...
a	Ah	Ah	T<u>a</u>co
e	Eh	Eh	<u>E</u>gg
i	Ih	I	<u>Ea</u>sy, F<u>ee</u>l
o	Oh	O	B<u>oo</u>k
u	Uh	U	B<u>u</u>ll
y	Yh	Y	S<u>y</u>llable
å	Åh	Å	B<u>o</u>rn
ä	Aeh	Aeh	B<u>a</u>d
ö	Öh	Ö	B<u>u</u>rn

Consonant Sounds

Consonant(s)	How to say the	How to pronounce	As in...

	letter	it in a word	
b	beh	similar to English b	<u>b</u>all
bb	n/a, occurs only within words.	similar to English b, preceeding vowel is short/hard.	<u>b</u>all
c	ceh	k before consonant s before vowel	<u>c</u>at <u>c</u>ereal
ck	n/a, occurs only within words.	k, preceeding vowel is short/hard.	<u>c</u>at
d	deh	a soft d (place your tongue at the back of your upper teeth)	ma<u>d</u>
dd	n/a, occurs only within words.	a hard d, preceeding vowel is short/hard.	<u>d</u>arling
f	efh	f	<u>f</u>ree
ff	n/a, occurs only within words.	a hard f, preceeding vowel is short/hard.	su<u>ff</u>er
g	geh	g before hard vowels j before soft vowels <u>sch</u> (see section 4 – Grammar School)	go <u>y</u>es bu<u>sh</u>
gg	n/a, occurs only within words.	a hard g, preceeding vowel is short/hard.	big
h	håh	h	<u>h</u>arvest
j	jih	j	bu<u>y</u>
jj	n/a, occurs only within words.	a hard g, preceeding vowel is short/hard.	la<u>y</u>er
<u>k</u>	Kåh	<u>k</u> initial k sometimes is pronounced "ch"	<u>k</u>arao<u>k</u>e <u>ch</u>icken
<u>kj</u>	n/a	Initial kj pronounced "ch"	<u>ch</u>icken

ḻ	ell	like English l with tongue raised to roof of mouth	la̱yer
ḻḻ	n/a, occurs only within words.	a hard l, preceeding vowel is short/hard.	mali̱cious
m	emh	m	mo̱ney
mm	n/a, occurs only within words.	a hard m, preceeding vowel is short/hard.	dummy
n	enn	n	no̱
nn	n/a, occurs only within words.	a hard n, preceeding vowel is short/hard.	nanny
p	peh	like English p	slope̱
pp	n/a, occurs only within words.	like English p	tap̱
q	kuh	k	qu̱ilt
r	ärr	rr, roll them	caṟ
rr	n/a, occurs only within words.	roll your r's as mentioned above	borrow
s	ess	Like English s	so̱rry
sj	n/a	Initial sj pronounced "sh"	bus̱h
sk	n/a	Initial sj pronounced "sh"	bus̱h
ss	n/a, occurs only within words.	Like English s, preceeding vowel is short/hard.	bus̱
t	teh	a soft English t, the tongue touches the back of the upper teeth	tu̱rn
tt	n/a, occurs only within words.	a hard t, preceeding vowel is short/hard.	bottom
v	veh	like English v	valv̱e
w	dubbelveh	like English w	w̱ater

x	ecks	*Between vowels and at the end of a word, it sounds like the English *ks*. *At the beginning of a word, it sounds like the letter *s*.	*bo<u>x</u> *<u>s</u>orry
z	säta	s	<u>s</u>ix

Note: If you're not sure how to pronounce a word, one thing you can do is type it in *Google translate* then click on the little speaker icon in the bottom left corner to hear the correct pronunciation.

Chapter 2
Swedish and English differences and Basic Grammar

We will now start with the most basic. I will explain some major things that are different between English and Spanish and some general Swedish grammar rules. Along with this, I will include basic vocabulary such as question words, numbers, colors, and other useful words and phrases to give you a foundation to help support you through the rest of this book. If you are trying to answer the practice questions in the following chapters and don't know how to say a vocabulary word, you will most likely find it in this chapter.

Note that this is to get you going. More elaboration and details in Swedish Grammar can be found in Section 4 – Grammar School. Much of the information found you will already have learnt bu it is on a more detailed and strict level.

Differences between English and Swedish

1.   Nouns: Nouns have two grammatical genders, common and neuter, which determine their definite forms as well as the form of any adjectives used to describe them. Noun gender is largely arbitrary and must be memorized; however, around three quarters of all Swedish nouns are common gender. Living beings are often common nouns, like in *en katt (a cat), en häst (a horse), en fluga (a fly)*, etc.

Swedish once had three genders - masculine, feminine and neuter. Though traces of the three-gender system still exist in archaic expressions and certain dialects, masculine and feminine nouns have today merged into the common gender, even if there are exceptions.

<u>**Common**</u> (n-words): "*-en*" is added to the noun to get definite form.

English	Swedish	Definite	Possessive pronoun	Plural	Plural definite	Plural possessive
King	Kung	Kung<u>en</u>	Kungen<u>s</u>	Kungar	Kungar<u>na</u>	Kungarna<u>s</u>
Car	Bil	Bil<u>en</u>	Bilen<u>s</u>	Bilar	Bilar<u>na</u>	Bilarna<u>s</u>
Moon	Måne	Måne<u>n</u> 1)	Månen<u>s</u>	Månar 2)	Månar<u>na</u>	Månarna<u>s</u>
Axe	Yxa	Yxan	Yxan<u>s</u>	Yxor 3)	Yxor<u>na</u>	Yxorna<u>s</u>
Sofa	Soffa	Soffan	Soffan<u>s</u>	Soffor	Soffor<u>na</u>	Sofforna<u>s</u>

1) When the noun ends with an "*a*" or "*e*" you only add the "*-n*" in definite form.
2) In plural when the noun ends with an "*e*" that letter should be replaced with "*-ar*".
3) The most common plural endings for n-words (common) are "*-or*", "*-ar*" and "*-er*". Nouns ending with a vowel, especially an "*a*" often ends with "*-or*" (with the "*a*" removed).

- Nouns ending with "*-are*" or "*-iker*" are unchanged in plural, e.g. *lärare* (teacher) and *magiker* (magician).

Neuter (t-words): "*-et*" is added to the noun to get definite form.

English	Swedish	Definite	Possessive pronoun	Plural	Plural definite	Plural possessive
Table	Bord	Bordet	Bordets	Bord 1)	Borden	Bordens
Train	Tåg	Tåget	Tågets	Tåg	Tågen	Tågens
Sea	Hav	Havet	Havets	Hav	Haven	Havens
Raspberry	Hallon	Hallonet	Hallonets	Hallon	Hallonen	Hallonens
Bee	Bi	Biet	Biets	Bin 2)	Bina	Binas

1) Nouns that end with a consonant usually have the same form in plural as in singular.
2) Nouns that end with a vowel usually ends with a "*–n*" plural form. Note: There are two exceptions – *Öga* (Eye) and *Öra* (Ear). Their plural forms are *Ögon* and *Öron* respectively.

- Neutrual nouns that ends with *–eri*, e.g. bag*eri* (bakery) ends with *-er* in plural i.e. bag*erier*.

2. Demonstrative pronouns: Here you find the translation of *this, that, these* and *those*. They are dependent on the grammatical gender of the noun (common or neuter) described above.

	Singular Indefinite	Singular Definite	Possessive pronoun	Plural Indefinite	Plural definite	Plural possessive
English	a/an	this, that	this, that	several	these, those	these, those
Swedish Common	en	den (här), den (där)	den (här), den (där)	flera	de (här), de (där)	de (här), de (där)
Swedish Neuter	ett	det (här), det (där)	det (här), det (där)	flera	de (här), de (där)	de (här), de (där)

3. Possessive pronouns: Possessive pronouns always relate to the indefinite form of the singular or plural form of the noun. They are dependent on the grammatical gender of the noun (common or neuter) described above.

		my	your	his	her	our	your	their
Swedish	Singular:	min	din	hans	hennes	vår	er	deras
Common	Plural:	mina	dina	hans	hennes	våra	era	deras
Swedish	Singular:	mitt	ditt	hans	hennes	vårt	ert	deras
Neuter	Plural:	mina	dina	hans	hennes	våra	era	deras

4. Plural forms: Nouns form the plural in a variety of ways. It is customary to classify regular Swedish nouns into five declensions based on their plural indefinite endings: -or, -ar, -er, -n, and unchanging nouns. See examples in "1. Nouns" above.

5. Articles and definite forms: The definite article in Swedish is mostly expressed by a suffix on the head noun, while the indefinite article is a separate word preceding the noun. This structure of the articles is shared by the Scandinavian languages. Articles differ in form depending on the gender and number of the noun. For details see examples in "1. Nouns" above and Section 4: Grammar School.

6. The genitive: The genitive is always formed by appending -s to the caseless form. In the second, third and fifth declensions words may end with an -s already in the caseless form. These words take no extra -s in genitive use: the genitive (indefinite) of hus ("house") is hus. See examples in "1. Nouns" above.

7. Adjective and Noun Agreement: Adjectives are words that describe or modify another person or thing in the sentence, eg red, big, strong, fat, beautiful, young and happy (*röd, stor, stark, tjock, vacker, ung, glad*). The adjectives must agree with the grammatical gender of the noun, common or neuter, and the number (singular or plural).

Examples:	**Positive**	**Comparative**	**Superlative**
English	Rich	Richer	Richest
Swedish	Rik	Rikare	Rikast

English	Hard	Harder	Hardest
Swedish	Hård	Hård<u>are</u>	Hård<u>ast</u>

English	Ugly	Uglier	Ugliest
Swedish	Ful	Ful<u>are</u>	Ful<u>ast</u>

English	Strong	Stronger	Strongest
Swedish	Stark	Stark<u>are</u>	Stark<u>ast</u>

So far so good. In comparative form you in Swedish add "-are" to the adjective and in superlative form you add "-ast". But certain adjectives have irregular form in comparative and superlative. This you more or less have to learn by heart.

English	bad	worse	worst
Swedish	dålig	sämre	sämst

English	little	less	least
Swedish	liten	mindre	minst

Below you see how the adjectives röd (red) and stor (large) relates to the grammatical genders, number and definite/indefinite form. As you can see it is rather straight forward.

	Common	Neuter
	1) Bil (Car)	1) Täcke (Blanket)
	2) Sten (Stone)	2) Bord (Table)
Indefinite **Singular**	1) En r<u>öd</u> bil	1) Ett r<u>ött</u> täcke
	2) En st<u>or</u> sten	2) Ett st<u>ort</u> bord
Definite **Singular**	1) Den röd<u>a</u> bilen	1) Det röd<u>a</u> täcket
	2) Den stor<u>a</u> stenen	2) Det stor<u>a</u> bordet
Indefinite **Plural**	1) Flera röd<u>a</u> bilar	1) Flera röd<u>a</u> täcken
	2) Flera stor<u>a</u> bord	2) Flera stor<u>a</u> bord
Definite **Plural**	1) De röd<u>a</u> bilarna	1) De röd<u>a</u> täckena
	2) De stor<u>a</u> borden	2) De stor<u>a</u> borden

8. Word Order: Unlike Spanish the word order in Swedish is most of the time the same as in English.

9. Verbs: Swedish verbs are mainly divided into two groups: Normal Verbs, Non-Continuous Verbs. Normal verbs are usually physical actions which you can see somebody doing. These verbs can be used in all tenses. Examples are *"att springa"* (to run), *"att äta"* (to eat), *"att flyga"* (to fly), *"att säga"* (to say), *"att röra"* (to touch). The group non-continuous verbs is smaller. These verbs are usually things you cannot see somebody doing. These verbs are rarely used in continuous tenses. They include *"att vilja"* (to want), *"att behöva"* (to need), *"att innehålla"* (to contain), *"att äga"* (to own), *"att existera"* (to exist), *"att tillhöra"* (to belong), *"att älska"* (to love).

As in English there also is a small Mixed Group. These verbs have more than one meaning.

English example:	Swedish example:
Nancy looks tired. (Non-Continuous Verb) (She seems tired). Farah is looking at the pictures. (Normal Verb) (She is looking with her eyes).	Jag vill gå härifrån. (I want to leave). Jag skall ut och gå. (I'm going out for a walk).

Tenses

English has three tenses: **the past**, **the present** and **the future** while Swedish have 5 tenses since Past Tense is divided into 3. Below you se examples för the words *"köpa"* (buy), *"äta"* (eat), *"måla"* (paint) and *"springa"* (run);

Tense	Description	Swedish	English
Presens	**Present tense.**	Köper, äter, målar, springer	Buying, eating, painting
Imperfekt	**Past tense.**	Köpte, åt, målade, sprang	Bought, ate, painted
Perfekt Aux. verb: *har*	**Past tense** for actions completed in the past.	Har köpt, ätit, målat, sprungit	Have/has bought, eaten, painted
Pluskvamperfekt Aux. verb: *hade*	**Past tense** for Action or state was completed before anything else happened.	Hade köpt, ätit, målat, sprungit	Had bought, eaten, painted
Futurum	**Future tense**	Ska	Will

Aux. verb: *ska, kommer att*		köpa, äta, måla, springa	buy, eat, paint

To-be

The different forms of the verb "to-be" is much simpler in Swedish than in English. See below;

Subject	Past tense	Present tense	Future tense
I (jag)	was	am	will be
You (du)	were	are	will be
He/She/It (Han/hon/det/den)	was	is	will be
We (vi)	were	are	will be
You (ni)	were	are	will be
They (de)	were	are	will be

In Swedish it is in all tenses they same word for all the subjects;

Jag/Du/han/den/ni/de etc.	var	är	kommer att vara

10. Formal You: There is a formal way to say *you* that is used to show respect to your elders or those in a higher position than you or simply for those whom you don't know well.

English	Informal Swedish	Formal Swedish
You	Du	Ni
Yours	Din	Er

11. Lack of Capitalization: Many words that are capitalized in English are not in Spanish. For example, days of the week, months, languages and nationalities.

Ex: Tuesday = tisdag, February = februari, Swedish = svenska, Italian = italienare.

12. Distance, length and weight: In Sweden they use the metric system which means that they e.g. instead of yards, miles, gallon and pound use meter, km (kilometer), liter (l) and kg (kilogram).

1 meter (m) = 1000 millimeter (mm), 100 centimer (cm), 10 decimeter (dm).

1 kilometer (km) = 1000 meter (m).
1 kilogram (kg) = 1000 gram (g)
1 liter (l) = 1000 milliliter (ml), 100 centiliter (cl), 10 deciliter (dl.)

Conversion table:

1 inch	25.4 mm
1 foot (12 inches)	304.8 mm
1 yard 3 feet, 36 inches	914.4 mm
1 mile	1.609 km
1 ounce	26.3 g
1 pound	453.6 g
1 fluid ounce	0.028 l
1 pint	0.568 l
1 gallon (4 pints)	4.546 l

Basic Grammar

Personal Pronouns

English	Swedish
I	jag
you	du
he, she, you	han, hon, ni
we	vi
they, you all	de, ni (alla)

Question Words

English	Swedish
What?	Vad?
Where?	Var?
When?	När?
Which?	Vilken?
Why?	Varför?
Who?	Vem?

Numbers 1-30

Numers 1-10		Numbers 11-20		Numers 21-30	
1	Ett	11	Elva	21	Tjugoett
2	Två	12	Tolv	22	Tjugotvå
3	Tre	13	Tretton	23	Tjugotre
4	Fyra	14	Fjorton	24	Tjugofyra
5	Fem	15	Femton	25	Tjugofem
6	Sex	16	Sexton	26	Tjugosex
7	Sju	17	Sjutton	27	Tjugosju
8	Åtta	18	Arton	28	Tjugoåtta
9	Nio	19	Nitton	29	Tjugonio
10	Tio	20	Tjugo	30	Trettio

After 30 this pattern is repeated.

Examples: 31= trettioett, 32 = trettiotvå, 57 = femtiosju, etc.

Numbers 30-1000

30	Trettio

200	Tvåhundra

40	Fyrtio		300	Trehundra
50	Femtio		400	Fyrahundra
60	Sextio		500	Femhundra
70	Sjuttio		600	Sexhundra
80	Åttio		700	Sjuhundra
90	Nittio		800	Åttahundra
100	Etthundra		900	Niohundra
105	Etthundrafem		999	Niohundranittionio
115	Etthundrafemton		1000	Ettusen

Here you can see a distinct continuous pattern, the same as in Englist. Under Chapter 4: Grammar School, Section 21: Numerals, you find much more about this.

Colors

English	Swedish
Red	Röd
Orange	Orange
Yellow	Gul
Green	Grön
Blue	Blå
Purple	Lila
Pink	Rosa
Black	Svart
White	Vit
Brown	Brun
Gray	Grå

Other useful vocabulary and phrases

English	Swedish
Yes	Ja
No	Nej
But	Men
also/too	Också
Is	Är
And	Och
An	En / Ett
In	In
With	Med

Or	Eller
Now	Nu
because	Eftersom
Well	Bra / Väl
Sorry	Ledsen
excuse me	Ursäkta (mig)
thank you	Tack
you're welcome	Varsågod
Please	Snälla / Vänligen (formal)
me too.	Jag/mig också
Very	Mycket
A lot	Många
That's okay/Okay	Det är okej / Okej

Hur är läget?

In this chapter we will go over the very necessary ways to greet and introduce yourself to others. Below is a list of common greetings in Spanish.

Common Greetings

English	Swedish
Hello	Hej
Good Morning	God morgon
Good Afternoon	Goddag
Good evening/Good night	Godkväll / Godnatt
General Greeting	Hej / Hejsan

Asking and Answering 'How are you?'

English	Swedish
How are you? (informal)	Hej / Hur är läget?
How are you? (formal)	Goddag / Hur står det till?
How are you doing? (informal)	Hej / Hur är läget?
How are you doing?(formal)	Goddag / Hur står det till?
How are you?	Hur är läget?
Well/Very well	Bra / Mycket bra
I feel excellent	Jag mår utmärkt
I feel bad	Jag mår dåligt
Good and you? (informal)	Bra, och du?
Good and you? (formal)	Bra tack, och du?
So-so	Sådär
What's up? What's new?	Läget? Något nytt?

Saying Goodbye

English	Spanish
Goodbye	Hej då / Adjö (formal)
See you later	(Vi) ses senare
See you tomorrow	(Vi) ses imorgon

See you soon	(Vi) ses snart
See you	(Vi) ses
Bye	Hej då

Exercises/Övningar!

Translate the following conversation into English #1:

Swedish	English translation
- Hej Peter!	
- God morgon Anna!	
- Hur är läget?	
- Mycket bra tack, och du?	
- Utmärkt, tack.	
- Vi ses senare Anna.	
- Vi ses Peter!	

*Did you notice there were some words that were not listed in the vocabulary above? Were you still able to use context clues and/or cognates (words that sound similar in both languages) and fill in the rest of the meaning as is suggested in the introduction? Remember, it is a great skill to have because most of the time there will be words that you may not understand in a conversation.

Introductions and Other phrases

English	Swedish
What is your name? (informal)	Vad heter du?
What is your name? (formal)	Vad heter Ni?
My name is…	Jag heter …
Nice to meet you!	Trevligt att träffas!

It's a pleasure.	Det är ett nöje.
Me too.	Ömsesidigt / Jag också.
Where are you from?	Varifrån kommer du?
I am from the U.S.	Jag kommer från USA.
How old are you?	Hur gammal är du?
I am... years old.	Jag är ... år (gammal).
Canada	Kanada
England	England
South Africa	Sydafrika
Australia	Australien

Cultural Note: **Kissing** --- In South European countries, people usually greet with a kiss on one cheek, or both cheeks. This is not common in Sweden.

*Below, I will list some useful phrases for when you don't understand, are confused, and need some clarification: a very common occurrence when learning a language.

Other Useful Phrases

English	Swedish
I don't understand.	Jag förstår inte.
Can you repeat, please.	Snälla, kan du upprepa.
Speak more slowly, please.	Snälla, prata lite långsammare.
How do you say ...?	Hur säger du ...?
What does this mean?	Vad betyder det här?
What is this?	Vad är det här?
Can you help me?	Kan du hjälpa mig?
Do you speak English?	Pratar du engelska?
I speak a little Swedish.	Jag pratar lite svenska.
I don't know.	Jag ve tinte.
Write it down, please.	Snälla, skriv ner det.

Exercises/Övningar!

Translate the following conversation into English #2:

Swedish	English translation
- Goddag!	

- Hej, hur är läget?	
- Bra tack, och du?	
- Sådär, tack.	
- Vad heter du?	
- Jag heter Eva, vad heter du?	
- Jag heter Bengt.	
- Hur gammal är du?	
- Jag är 25 år gammal, och du?	
- Jag är 29 år gammal, varifrån kommer du?	
- Jag kommer från Kanada, varifrån kommer du?	
- Jag kommer från Colombia.	
- Trevligt att träffas!	
- Det var ett nöje för mig också! / Det samma!	

Match the Phrases:

English	↓		Swedish	
1. I speak a little Swedish.		a.	Vad betyder det här?
2. Write it down, please.		b.	Jag pratar lite svenska.
3. Do you speak English?		c.	Jag vet inte.
4. I don't understand.		d.	Snälla, prata långsamt.
5. How do you say…?		e.	Vad är det här?

6. I don't know.		f.	Snälla, skriv ner det.
7. Speak slowly please.		g.	Pratar du engelska?
8. Can you repeat, please?		h.	Jag förstår inte.
9. What is this?		i.	Snälla, kan du upprepa?
10. What does this mean?		j.	Hur säger du …?

Chapter 3 Answers

Translation #1:

Swedish	English translation
- Hej Peter!	- Hi Peter!
- God morgon Anna!	- Good morning, Anna!
- Hur är läget?	- How's it going?
- Mycket bra tack, och du?	- Very good, thanks. And you?
- Utmärkt, tack.	- Excellent, thanks.
- Vi ses senare Anna.	- See you later, Anna.
- Vi ses Peter!	- See you, Peter!

Translation #2:

Swedish	English translation
- Goddag!	- Good afternoon!
- Hej, hur är läget?	- Hi! How are you?
- Bra tack, och du?	- Good, thanks. And you?
- Sådär, tack.	- So so, thank you.
- Vad heter du?	- What's your name?
- Jag heter Eva, vad heter du?	- My name is Eva, and you what is your name?
- Jag heter Bengt.	- My name is Bengt.
- Hur gammal är du?	- How old are you?
- Jag är 25 år gammal, och du?	- I am 25 years old and you?
- Jag är 29 år gammal, varifrån kommer du?	- I'm 29 years old. Where are you from?
- Jag kommer från Kanada. Varifrån kommer du?	- I am from Canada. Where are you from?
- Jag kommer från Colombia.	- I am from Colombia
- Trevligt att träffas!	- Nice to meet you!
- Det var ett nöje för mig också! / Det samma!	- It's a pleasure for me too! / The same

Match the Phrases:

English		Swedish
1. I speak a little Swedish.	b.	Jag pratar lite svenska.
2. Write it down, please.	f.	Snälla, skriv ner det.
3. Do you speak English?	g.	Pratar du engelska?
4. I don't understand.	h.	Jag förstår inte.

5. How do you say…?	j.		Hur säger du …?
6. I don't know.	c.		Jag vet inte.
7. Speak slowly please.	d.		Snälla, prata långsamt.
8. Can you repeat, please?	i.		Snälla, kan du upprepa?
9. What is this?	e.		Vad är det här?
10. What does this mean?	a.		Vad betyder det här?

Chapter 4
About Time - Telling time, Days of Week, Dates

In this chapter, I will discuss how to talk about time, telling time, days of week, months, etc.

Unlike the relaxed attitude to time in Latin-American cultures, keeping the time is very important in Sweden. In everything from business to school it is considered very rude to be more than 15 minutes late. Below I have several useful phrases to talk about time.

Note. In English you tend to say e.g. *"half three"* when you mean *"half past three"*. This can create confusion since half three (*halv tre*) equals 30 minutes **to** 3 in Swedish. Also, in Sweden you don't use a.m./p.m., only 00.00-24.00h is used. However, when the time is 14.00 you say that it is 2 when it's obvious. 15 minutes translates into *"en kvart"* (quarter) and time is considered feminine so when you ask the time the answer could be *"hon är kvart i åtta"* (she is a quarter to eight).

Telling Time

English	Swedish
What time is is?	Vad är klockan?
It's one.	Hon är ett.
It's two.	Hon är två
It's four thirty.	Hon är halv fem.
It's fifteen until eight.	Hon är kvart i åtta.
a.m. (in the morning)	På morgonen
p.m. (in the afternoon)	På eftermiddagen
p.m. (at night)	På kvällen/natten

* If you want to add minutes to the hour just use the word '*över*' *when it is past and* '*i*' *when it is (un)til.*

> **Ex:** It is 6:05 = Hon är fem över sex
> It is 10:40 = Hon är tjugo i elva
> It is 11:45 = Hon är kvart i tolv

Now you try:

English	Swedish translation
1. It is 3:05	
2. It is 10:45	
3. It is 8:20	
4. It is fifteen til three.	
5. It is five til seven.	
6. It is ten til nine.	

Days of the Week

English	Swedish
What day is today?	Vilken dag är det idag?
Today is Thursday	Idag är det torsdag
Today	idag
Yesterday	igår
Tomorrow	I morgon
Monday	måndag
Tuesday	tisdag
Wednesday	onsdag
Thursday	torsdag
Friday	fredag
Saturday	lördag
Sunday	söndag

As mentioned before, Swedish does not typically capitalize the days of the weeks.

Talking about the Date

English	Swedish
What is the date today?	Vad är dagens datum?
Today is February 15th	Idag är det den 15:e februari
January	januari
February	februari

March	mars
April	april
May	maj
June	juni
July	juli
August	augusti
September	september
October	oktober
November	november
December	december

* As indicated above Swedish date format is reversed. February 15th is "*15:e februari*" in Swedish. Also, the English mm/dd/yyyy is åååå-mm-dd in Swedish.

* Swedish does not typically capitalize months.

Exercises/Övningar!

Translate to Swedish using only letter:

English	Swedish translation
1. It is 3:05	
2. It is 10:45	
3. It is 8:20	
4. It is fifteen til three.	
5. It is five til seven.	
6. It is ten til nine.	

Choose a correct answer:

7. Vad är klockan? _____

a. Det är eftermiddag	b. Hon är halv fyra
c. Det är februari	d. Hon är kvar

8. Vad är det för dag idag? _____

a. Tomorrow is Monday	b. Today is Friday
c. Yesterday was Sunday	d. It is June

9. Today is March 27th. _____

a. 27:e Mars är en torsdag	b. Idag är det mars 27:e
c. Idag är det 27:e mars	d. Idag är det 27:e maj

10. It is ten til seven. _____

a. Hon är tio i sju	b. Hon är sju i tio
c. Det är den 10:e i sjunde	d. Hon är tio över sju

11. It is 3:15. _____

a. Hon är kvart i tre	b. Hon är 15 minuter i 3
c. Det är den 15:e mars	d. Hon är kvart över tre

Chapter 4 Answers

Now you try:

English	Swedish translation
1. It is 3:05	Hon är fem över tre
2. It is 10:45	Hon är kvart i elva
3. It is 8:20	Hon är tjugo över åtta
4. It is fifteen til three.	Hon är kvart i tre.
5. It is five til seven.	Hon är fem i sju.
6. It is ten til nine.	Hon är tio i nio.

Choose the correct answer:

7. Vad är klockan?	b. Hon är halv fyra
8. Vad är det för dag idag?	b. Today is Friday
9. Today is March 27th	c. Idag är det 27:e mars
10. It is ten til seven	a. Hon är tio i sju
11. It is 3:15	d. Hon är kvart över tre

Chapter 5
How Do You Like This Weather?

Vad är det för väder?

This chapter will discuss how to talk about the weather, something people often talk about when there is nothing else to talk about. It also is useful information to have, as in these days it can be perfectly sunny one moment and then torrentially raining, the next. Below are some useful phrases and vocabulary to use when talking about the weather.

Weather Expressions

English	Swedish
What's the weather like today?	Hur är vädret idag?
It is cold	Det är kallt
It is hot	Det är varmt
It is sunny	Det är soligt
It is windy	Det är blåsigt
The weather is nice	Vädret är fint/bra
The weather is bad	Vädret är dåligt
It's cool.	Det är kallt.
It's raining.	Det regnar.
Is it going to rain today?	Kommer det att regna idag?
Yes, it's going to rain. No, it's not going to rain	Ja, det kommer att regna. Nej, det kommer inte att regna.
It's snowing	Det snöar
Really?	Verkligen?

Exercises/Övningar!

Choose the correct answer:

1. Vad är det för väder idag? _____

a. Det blåste igår	b. Det kan regna imorgon
c. Det regnar och är kallt	d. Det kan vara kallt om det regnar

2. It is very sunny today. _____

a. Solen skiner på dagen	b. Det är mycket soligt idag

c. Det kan vara soligt idag	d. Det blir ingen sol idag

3. Kommer det att regna idag? _____

a. Ja, det snöar mycket	b. Det är kallt och blåsigt
c. Det kommer att regna imorgon	d. Ja, det kommer att regna idag

Translate to Swedish:

English	Swedish translation
- Hi friend, how are you?	
- Good! How is the weather today?	
- It's nice! It's not going to rain.	
- But, it is very windy.	
- Yes, but very sunny too.	
- See you tomorrow!	
- Goodbye!	

Chapter 5 Answers

Choose the correct answer:

1. Vad är det för väder idag?	c. Det regnar och är kallt
2. It is very sunny today.	b. Det är mycket soligt idag
3. Kommer det att regna idag?	d. Ja, det kommer att regna idag.

Translation:

English	Swedish translation
- Hi friend, how are you? - Good! How is the weather today? - It's nice! It's not going to rain. - But, it is very windy. - Yes, but very sunny too. - See you tomorrow! - Goodbye!	- Hej vännen, hur mår du? - Bra! Hur är vädret idag? - Det är fint! Det kommer inte att regna. - Men, det är mycket blåsigt. - Ja, med det är mycket soligt också. - Vi ses imorgon! - Hej då!

SECTION 2
IN THE CITY AND TRAVELLING

Var ligger banken?

Now, we will move onto some more very useful everyday vocabulary, especially if you are in a new country and have no idea where anything is. Now, these days with google maps and GPS, stopping to ask for directions is less common. However, you will not allways have easy access to internet while you are on the streets at least. So get ready to have to actually talk to people face to face and maybe occasionally get a little lost. Below I have some of the most useful phrases and vocabulary for getting around in Swedish.

Phrases to talk about Directions

English	Swedish
Where is it?	Var ligger det? [1]
Excuse me, where is the…	Ursäkta mig, var ligger …
It's next to the…	Det/den ligger bredvid …
It's in front of the…	Det/den ligger framför …
Keep straight	Fortsätt rakt fram
Turn right	Sväng höger
Turn left	Sväng vänster
It's on the right/left	Det/den ligger på höger/vänster sida
Far from	Långt ifrån
Near to	Nära
Above	Över
Below	Under
Behind	Bakom

1) "Where is it" translates to "Var är det?" if it referes to a thing/item. When it referes to a location the translation is "Var ligger det?".

Places

English	Swedish
The bank	Banken
The restaurant	Restaurangen
The post office	Postkontoret
The supermarket	Affären/Stormarknaden

The pharmacy	Apoteket
The bakery	Bageriet
Bus/Train station	Busstationen/Tågstationen
Store	Affär
Church	Kyrka
Stationary Store	Bokhandel[1]

1) *"Bokhandel"* more referrers to "bookstore" but that's where they sell stationary items.

*Note that in Swedish you add *"–en"* or *"–et"* to the noun to indicate definite form (the).

Other Phrases

English	Swedish
I am lost.	Jag är vilse.
How do I get to ...?	Hur kommer jag till ...?
Cross the street.	Gå över gatan.
Where am I now?	Var är jag nu?
the corner	hörnet
one block	ett kvarter
street	gata
here	här
there	där
there	där borta (farther away)

Time Expressions

English	Swedish
Before	Före
Now	Nu
After	Efter
Later/Then	Senare / Då

Exercises/Övningar!

Choose the correct answer:

1. The bank is next to the post office.

a. Postkontoret ligger vid sidan om banken	b. Banken ligger bakom postkontoret
c. Banken ligger bredvid postkontoret	d. Banken ligger nära postkontoret

2. Turn right at the bakery.

a. Sväng höger vid bageriet.	b. Sväng höger bakom bageriet
c. Sväng rätt vid bageriet	d. Sväng vänster vid bageriet

3. The store is close to the church.

a. Affären ligger bredvid kyrkan.	b. Kyrkan ligger nära affären.
c. Affären och kyrkan ligger på samma gata.	d. Affären ligger nära kyrkan.

Translate to English:

Swedish	English translation
- Ursäkta mig, var ligger tågstationen?	
- Fortsätt rakt fram och sväng vänster vid hörnet.	
- Ok.	
- Fortsätt sedan att gå tre kvarter.	
- Ok.	
- och gå över gatan så ligger den bredvid bokhandeln.	
- Är det mycket långt?	
- Nej, det är inte mycket långt.	
- Ok, tack så mycket.	

- Varsågod, vi ses senare.	

Chapter 6 Answers

Choose the correct answer:

1. The bank is next to the post office.	c. Banken ligger bredvid postkontoret
2. Turn right at the bakery.	a. Sväng höger vid bageriet.
3. The store is close to the church.	d. Affären ligger nära kyrkan.

Translation:

Swedish	English translation
- Ursäkta mig, var ligger tågstationen? - Fortsätt rakt fram och sväng vänster vid hörnet. - Ok. - Sedan, fortsätt att gå tre kvarter. - Ok. - och gå över gatan så ligger den bredvid bokhandeln. - Är det mycket långt? - Nej, det är inte mycket långt. - Ok, tack så mycket. - Varsågod, vi ses senare.	- Excuse me, where is the train station? - Keep straight and turn left at the corner. - Ok. - Then, keep going for three blocks. - Ok - and cross the street and it's next to the stationary store. - Is it very far? - No, it's not very far. - Ok/well, thank you very much! - Your welcome, see you later.

Hur mycket kostar det?

Now, let's move onto a very enjoyable (usually) and common activity that we do in other countries- shopping! Sweden is of course famous for IKEA but those stores you have at home. Some other popular products from Swedan are crystal, jewelry, art, gravlax (raw spiced salmon), lingonberry jam and candy, especially licorice. Whether it be shopping for cheesy souvenirs for your friends and family or shopping for some stylish local clothes for yourself, we've got the basics to help you bargain around and hopefully find what you are looking for. Remember that bargaining is not very common in Sweden, but at local markets and in antique- and second hand shops you might be lucky. So, let's see if we can find you a great deal!

Shopping phrases

English	Swedish
How can I help you?	Kan jag hjälpa till?
How much does it cost?	Hur mycket kostar den/det?
How much is it?	Hur mycket blir det?
Which one do you want?	Vilken vill du ha?
I would like that one.	Jag vill ha den.
It's too expensive.	Det är för dyrt.
Do you have...?	Har du ...?
Do you have bigger/smaller?	Har du större / mindre?
Do you accept credit cards?	Tar ni kreditkort?
We only accept cash.	Vi tar bara kontanter.
Can I try it on?	Kan jag prova den?
I'm just looking.	Jag bara tittar.
Of course!	Självklart!

Shopping Vocabulary

English	Swedish
buy	köpa
sell	sälja
souvenirs	souvenirer
clothes	kläder

shirt	skjorta
pants	byxor
shorts	kortbyxor
a dress	en klänning
a jacket	en jacka/kavaj
shoes	skor
cap	keps / mössa
keychain	nyckelring
coffee	kaffe
tea	te
milk	mjölk
juice	juice
water	vatten
bread	bröd
butter	smör
cheese	ost
ham	skinka
egg	ägg

Below, I will list the demonstrative adjectives in Swedish (this, that, these, those) as they are very useful to use when shopping, 'I would like that one, please.'

Demonstrative Adjectives (This, That, These, Those)

This and That

English	Swedish
This	Den/det här
That	Den/det där
These	De här
Those	De där

Exercises/Övningar!

Translate to English:

Swedish	English translation

- God morgon, hur kan jag hjälpa till?	
- Jag bara tittar, tack.	
- Varsågod.	
- Hur mycket kostar den här klänningen?	
- Åttahundra kronor	
- Det är mycket dyrt! Och dom här byxorna?	
- Trehundrafyrtiofem kronor	
- Kan jag prova dom?	
- Självklart	
- Tar ni kreditkort?	
- Nej, vi acceterar bara kontanter.	
- Okej, tack så mycket.	

Translate to Swedish:

English	Swedish translation
- Good evening, how are you?	
- I'm fine thank you! How are you?	
- So so, thank you. What is that?	
- It's my new computer.	
- Then you might whant these CDs.	
- How much are they?	

- You can have them for free!	
- Thanks mate!	
- You are welcome! Bye.	

Chapter 7 Answers

Translation to English:

Swedish	English translation
- God morgon, hur kan jag hjälpa till?	- Good morning, how can I help you?
- Jag bara tittar, tack.	- I'm just looking, thanks.
- Varsågod.	- Your welcome.
- Hur mycket kostar den här klänningen?	- How much does this dress cost?
- Åttahundra kronor	- 800 kronor.
- Det är mycket dyrt! Och dom här byxorna?	- It's very expensive! And these pants?
- Trehundrafyrtiofem kronor	- 345 kronor.
- Kan jag prova dom?	- Can I try them on?
- Självklart	- Of course!
- Tar ni kreditkort?	- Do you accept credit cards?
- Nej, vi acceterar bara kontanter.	- No, we only accept cash.
- Okej, tack så mycket.	- Okay, thank you very much.

Translation to Swedish:

English	Swedish translation
- Good evening, how are you?	- Godkväll, hur mår du?
- I'm fine thank you! How are you?	- Tack, jag mår bra! Hur mår du?
- So so, thank you. What is that?	- Tack, sådär. Vad är det där?
- It's my new computer.	- Det är min nya dator.
- Then you might whant these CDs.	- Då kanske du vill ha dom här CD-skivorna.
- How much are they?	- Hur mycket kostar dom?
- You can have them for free!	- Du kan få dom gratis!
- Thanks mate!	- Tack kompis!
- You are welcome! Bye.	- Varsågod! Hej då.

Kan jag få menyn tack?

In this chapter we will discuss another common and delicious activity- going out to eat in restaurants. In Sweden you can find delicious cuisines from all over the world. The Swedes almost even claim that pizza was invented in Sweden. You should specify if you want your water carbonated (kolsyrat) or regular (utan kolsyra). Tipping is common in finer restaurants and evening dinners but not for lunch. The water in Sweden is so clean that you without any problem can ask for tap water. Let's get ready to eat! Bon Appetite or as they say in Sweden, *Smaklig måltid!*

Restaurant phrases

English	Swedish
What can I bring you?	Vad önskas?
I would like to eat...	Jag skulle vilja äta...
I would like to drink...	Jag skulle vilja dricka...
Menu, please	Skulle jag kunna få menyn?
What do you recommend?	Vad rekommenrerar ni?
Can you bring me...?	Skulle jag kunna få...?
What can I bring you?	Vad önskas?
Excuse me, sir	Ursäkta mig[1]
Excuse me, ma'am	Ursäkta mig[1]
Beverage	Dryck
A glass	Ett glas
Soft Drink	Läst / alkoholfri dryck
Juice	Juice
A glass of water	Ett glas vatten
A beer	En öl
A glass of (red/white) wine	Ett glas (rött/vitt) vin
Drink	Drink
Dessert	Dessert
It was very delicious	Det var mycket gott
Tip	Dricks
(can I have the) check, please	(skulle jag kunna få) notan, tack

1) Sir and ma'am not used in Swedish in daily speech.

Food Vocabulary

English	Swedish
What does this dish have?	Vad består den här rätten av? [1]
Does this dish have...?	Innehåller den här rätten...? [1]
Meat	Kött
Fish	Fisk
Chicken	Kyckling
Ham	Skinka
Egg	Ägg
Pasta	Pasta
Salad	Sallad
Bread	Bröd
Cheese	Ost
Vegetables	Grönsaker
Breakfast	Frukost
Lunch	Lunch
Dinner	Middag
There is/there are	Both *"Det finns"* and *"Där är"* works in either case.

[1] ...this dish have... can be said in two ways. Speaking about the ingredients you say *"innehåller"* (contains), and when you refer to the composition you say *"består av"*.

Exercises/Övningar!

Choose the correct answer:

1. This dish has fish, vegetables, and bread.

a. Den här rätten består av fisk, veganer och bröd.	b. Den här disken består av fisk, grönsaker och bröd.
c. Den här rätten består av ost, smör och bröd.	d. Den här rätten består av fisk, grönsaker och bröd.

2. Can you bring me a beer please?

a. Skulle jag kunna få en öl tack?	b. Skulle jag kunna få notan tack?
c. Skulle jag kunna få mer öl?	d. Skulle jag kunna få ett glas vin tack?

3. Excuse me ma'am, the check please.

| a. Ursäkta mig, tar ni checkar? | b. Varsågod, här har ni en check. |
| c. Ursäkta mig, jag kan inte betala notan. | d. Ursäkta mig, skulle jag kunna få notan? |

4. Till frukost är det bröd, ost och ägg.

| a. For lunch there is bread, cheese, | b. For breakfast there is fish, ham, |
| c. For breakfast there is bread, cheese, and eggs. | d. For dinner there is ham, eggs, and bread. |

5. Efter middagen skulle jag vilja ha dessert.

| a. Before lunch, I would like dessert. | b. After dinner, I would like dessert. |
| c. After dinner, I would like wine . | d. After lunch, I would like dessert. |

Translate to English:

Swedish	English translation
- Godkväll. Vad önskas?	
- Godkväll, vad rekommenderar ni?	
- Den här rätten består av kött, grönsaker och bröd, och den är mycket god.	
- Okej, då skulle jag vilja ha den.	
- Och att dricka?	
- Jag skulle vilja ha ett glas vin tack.	

- Okej.	
- Tack så mycket.	

Chapter 8 Answers

Choose the correct answer:

1. This dish has fish, vegetables and bread.	d. Den här rätten innehåller fisk, grönsaker och bröd.
2. Can you bring me a beer please?	a. Skulle jag kunna få en öl tack?
3. Excuse me ma'am, the check please.	d. Ursäkta mig, skulle jag kunna få notan?
4. Till frukost är det bröd, ost och ägg.	c. For breakfast there is bread, cheese, and eggs.
5. Efter middagen skulle jag vilja ha dessert.	b. After dinner, I would like dessert.

Translation to English:

Swedish	English translation
- Godkväll. Vad önskas? - Godkväll, vad rekommenderar ni? - Den här rätten består av kött, grönsaker och bröd, och den är mycket god. - Okej, då skulle jag vilja ha den. - Och att dricka? - Jag skulle vilja ha ett glas vin tack. - Okej. - Tack så mycket.	- Good evening. What can I bring you? - Good evening, what can you recommend? - This dish has meat, vegetables and bread, and is very delicious. - Okay, I would like that dish then. - And to drink? - I would like a glass of wine please. - Okay. - Thank you, sir/ma'am.

Jag känner mig dålig.

Let's talk about a not so fun but absolutely necessary event that you should be prepared for, going to the doctor or the hospital. Getting sick is no fun and even more difficult to deal with when you don't know how to communicate how you are feeling or what is wrong with you. It also can be a very likely event when you are in another country as you are eating food and are exposed to germs both of which your body is not used to. I remember living in Chile and becoming very ill after eating a traditional Chilean dish that is cooked in the ground and includes a mix of shellfish, meats, and sausages. I was taken to the hospital and would have definitely found the following phrases to be very useful. Below are some very basic and useful phrases to use when you are sick, going to the doctor, or hospital.

Phrases to use at the Doctor

English	Swedish
What's wrong?	Vad är felet?
I am sick.	Jag är sjuk.
I have a cold.	Jag är förkyld.
I have a headache.	Jag har huvudvärk.
Sore throat	Ont i halsen.
You should rest.	Du borde vila.
Injection	Spruta
Cough	Hosta
Fever	Feber
Medicine	Medicin
Prescription	Recept
Here is ...	Här är ...
Do you have health insurance?	Har du sjukförsäkring?

More Doctor Visit Vocabulary

English	Swedish
Where does it hurt?	Var gör det ont?
It hurts here.	Det gör ont här
My ... hurts.	Mitt/min ... gör ont.
Head	Huvud

Arm	Arm
Leg	Ben
Stomach	Mage
Hand	Hand
Foot	Fot
Eyes	Ögon
Nose	Näsa
Mouth	Mun
Ear/Inner ear	Öra / Inneröra
Chest	Bröst / Bröstkorg
I have diarrhea	Jag har diarré
I have been vomiting	Jag har kräkts

Exercises/Övningar!

Translate to Swedish:

English	Swedish translation
- His arm hurts.	
- My foot hurts.	
- Does your head hurt?	
- Her chest hurts.	
- Where does it hurt?	

Match the Vocabulary:

English	↓		Swedish
1. arm		a.	fot
2. chest		b.	öra
3. foot		c.	ögon
4. hand		d.	mun
5. ear		e.	arm
6. eyes		f.	huvud
7. leg		g.	mage
8. mouth		h.	ben
9. stomach		i.	bröst
10. head		j.	hand

Translate to English:

Swedish	English translation
- God eftermiddag, vad är det för fel idag?	
- Jag är förkyld och har huvudvärk.	
- Har du hosta eller ont i halsen?	
- Ja, jag har hosta och lite ont i halsen.	
- Du har inte feber. Här är ett recept.	
- Tack.	
- Har du sjukförsäkring?	
- Ja, det har jag.	
- Okej. Du måste vila mycket.	
- Ja visst. Tack så mycket.	
- Varsågod, vi ses senare.	

Chapter 9 Answers

Translation to Swedish:

English	Swedish translation
- His arm hurts.	- Hans arm gör ont.
- My foot hurts.	- Min fot gör ont.
- Does your head hurt?	- Har du ont i huvudet?
- Her chest hurts.	- Hennes bröst gör ont.
- Where does it hurt?	- Var gör det ont?

Match the Vocabulary:

English		Swedish
1. arm	e.	arm
2. chest	i.	bröst
3. foot	a.	fot
4. hand	j.	hand
5. ear	b.	öra
6. eyes	c.	ögon
7. leg	h.	ben
8. mouth	d.	mun
9. stomach	g.	mage
10. head	f.	huvud

Translation to English:

Swedish	English translation
- God eftermiddag, vad är det för fel idag?	- Good afternoon, what's wrong today?
- Jag är förkyld och har huvudvärk.	- I have a cold and headache.
- Har du hosta eller ont i halsen?	- Do you have a cough or sore throat?
- Ja, jag har hosta och lite ont i halsen.	- Yes I have a cough and a little bit of a sore throat.
	- You don't have a fever. Here is a prescription.
- Du har inte feber. Här är ett recept.	
- Tack.	- Thank you.
- Har du sjukförsäkring?	- Do you have health insurance?
- Ja, det har jag.	- Yes, I do.
	- Okay. You should get a lot of rest.

- Okej. Du måste vila mycket. - Ja visst. Tack så mycket. - Varsågod, vi ses senare.	- Yes, sir. Thank you very much. - Your welcome, see you later.

Jag behöver ta ut pengar

In this chapter we will discuss something that you definitely want to be well-informed on so that you don't make any major mistakes when dealing with your money. When you are traveling, studying, or working abroad you may choose to use a credit card, travelers cheques, an atm card, or to open your own bank account. In any of these cases, you will probably have to deal with going to the bank at least once during your stay, whether it is to transfer money home, withdraw, or exchange money. Below are some very useful phrases for you to deal with your money in Sweden.

Banking Phrases

English	Swedish
I need to withdraw money	Jag behöver ta ut pengar
Deposit money	Sätta in pengar
Exchange money	Växla pengar
How much is the dollar worth? Whats is the dollar exchange rate?	Hur mycket är en dollar värd? Vad är dollarkursen?
I want to open an account.	Jag vill öppna ett konto.
I want to transfer money.	Jag vill överföra pengar.
Cash	Kontanter
Currency	Valuta

Vocabulary – At the bank

English	Swedish
Credit Card	Kreditkort
Debet Card	Betalkort
Traveler's cheques	Resecheckar
Account	Konto
Cashier	Kassör (male) / Kassörska (female)
ATM	Bankomat
Loan	Lån
Identification (ID)	Identifikation (Id)
Amount	Belopp

Exercises/Övningar!

Match the Vocabulary:

Swedish	↓		English	
1. belopp		a.	loan	
2. kontanter		b.	credit card	
3. bankomat		c.	amount	
4. att växla		d.	cashier	
5. resecheckar		e.	currency	
6. lån		f.	ATM	
7. konto		g.	cash	
8. kreditkort		h.	to exchange	
9. betalkort		i.	traveler's cheques	
10. valuta		j.	account	
11. kassör		k.	debet card	

Translate to English:

Swedish	English translation
- Hej, hur kan jag hjälpa till?	
- Hejsan, jag behöver växla pengar.	
- Okej.	
- Hur mycket är dollarn värd?	
- Dollar är värd sex kronor.	
- Okej, jag vill växla etthundra dollar.	
- Här är sexhundra kronor.	
- Tack så mycket.	
- Varsågod.	

Chapter 10 Answers

Match the Vocabulary:

Swedish		English
1. belopp	c.	amount
2. kontanter	g.	cash
3. bankomat	f.	ATM
4. att växla	h.	to exchange
5. resecheckar	i.	traveler's cheques
6. lån	a.	loan
7. konto	j.	account
8. kreditkort	b.	credit card
9. betalkort	k.	debet card
10. valuta	e.	currency
11. kassör	d.	cashier

Translation to English:

Swedish	English translation
- Hej, hur kan jag hjälpa till?	- Hello, how can I help you?
- Hejsan, jag behöver växla pengar.	- Hi, I need to exchange money.
- Okej.	- Okay.
- Hur mycket är dollarn värd?	- How much is the dollar worth?
- Dollar är värd sex kronor.	- The dollar is worth 6 kronor.
- Okej, jag vill växla etthundra dollar.	- Okay, I want to exchange 100 dollars.
- Här är sexhundra kronor.	- Here is 600 kronor.
- Tack så mycket.	- Thank you very much.
- Varsågod.	- Your welcome.

Vart är vi på väg?

Part 1: At the airport

This chapter will be divided into two sections: *At the Airport* and *Travelling by taxi, bus or train.* This section is dedicated to that ever exciting moment of arriving in the airport of the new country where you will study, play, sightsee, work or whatever your motive may be. It is true that most airport employees speak rather good English but in some cases, it might be limited so it is always helpful if you are one step ahead and know how to say a few useful things to get you through customs, outside of the airport, and ready to embark on your new adventure. Bon voyage or as they say in Swedish *"Trevlig resa"*!

At the Airport

English	Swedish
Airport	Flygplats
Airplane	Flygplan
Airline	Flygbolag
Suitcase	Resväska
Passport	Pass
Flight	Flyg / Flight
Customs	Tull
Ticket	Biljett
Baggage Claim Area	Bagageutlämning
Gate	Gate
Leave	Avgår
Arrive	Ankommer
Terminal	Terminal
Destination	Destination
Have a nice trip!	Ha en trevlig resa!

An airport is a very international environment so many of the Swedish words are similar to their English counterpart, as you can see above.

Useful Phrases at the Airport

English	Swedish
When does the flight leave?	När avgår flyget?
When does the flight arrive?	När ankommer flyget?
I have two suitcases.	Jag har två resväskor.
Where is terminal B?	Var ligger terminal B?
I´m looking for gate 17.	Jag letar efter gate 17.
Where is the baggage claim?	Var är bagageutlämningen?
My suitcases are lost.	Jag har förlorat mina resväskor.

Exercises/Övningar!

Fill in the blanks with the words from the word bank:

resväska	Flight 312	biljett	bagageutlämningen	terminal	tullen

1. I vilken _____ ligger gate 14?

2. Nu ska jag hämta min _____ i

_____ .

3. När jag hämtat väskan måste jag gå igenom _____.

4. Hur mycket kostade din _____ till England?

5. Jag ska till Sverige med SAS _____ klockan 7.

Match the Vocabulary:

Swedish	↓		English	
6. Flygplan		a.	Airline	
7. Ha en trevlig resa.		b.	Ticket	
8. Biljett		c.	Airplane	
9. Flygbolag		d.	Have a nice trip.	

Translate to English:

Swedish	English translation

- Hej, hur kan jag hjälpa till?	
- Hej, när avgår flyget till Buenos Aires?	
- Det avgår kl. 15.00.	
- Vilken gate avgår det från?	
- Från gate tio i terminal två.	
- Okej, tack så mycket.	
- Varsågod, trevlig resa!	

Part 2: Travelling by taxi, bus, or train.

This section is dedicated to that travelling you will do within the city or from city to city in your new country. Knowing how to read the signs and ask around inside of the various bus and train stations will hopefully help you avoid getting completely lost. And if you do, it will help you to get out of the situation. I always suggest being flexible and ready for adventure because sometimes getting lost just means you get to experience a completely new scenery you´ve never seen before. Within the city you may travel by bus, or taxi. Travelling by taxi is usually an excellent way to get language practice as you have your own personal conversation partner until you arrive to your destination. You will most likely travel by bus or train to go from city to city. Happy exploring in your new country!

Taxi Vocabulary

English	Swedish
Where are we going?	Vart ska vi?
I'm going to...	Jag skall till ...
At the stoplight, turn right/left	Sväng höger vid rödljuset[1]
You can stop here.	Du kan stanna här.
Here on the right/left	Här till höger/vänster
How much do I owe you?	Hur mycket är jag skyldig?

1) "Stoplight" translates through the color of the light when you should stop, i.e. red light translates to "*rödljus*".

Exercises/Övningar!

Match the Phrases:

Swedish	↓	English
1. Du kan stanna här		a. Here on the right.
2. Sväng vänster vid rödljuset		b. How much do I owe you?
3. Hur mycket är jag skyldig?		c. You can stop here
4. Vart ska vi?		d. Where are we going?
5. Här till höger.		e. At the stoplight, turn left.

Translate (#1):

English	Swedish translation
- I'm going to Malmö, how much is it?	
- It's around SEK 300-.	
- Okay, let's go.	
- Where in Malmö do you want to go?	
- To the train station please.	
- Turn left here.	
- Okay, here it is.	
- Thank you. Here you have 350 kronor, keep the change.	
- Thank you very much, goodbye ma'am.	

Bus and Train Vocabulary

English	Swedish
The bus/train station	Busstationen / Tågstationen
Bus stop	Busshållplats
When does the next train leave for...?	När går nästa tåg till...?
Departures	Avgångar
Arrivals	Ankomster
I would like a one way ticket	Jag skulle vilja ha en enkelbiljett
Round trip ticket	Tur & Retur [1]
Which platform does the train leave from?	Vilken platform avgår tåget från?
Do I need to change trains?	Behöver jag byta tåg?
To get on...	Att gå på...
To get off..	Att gå av...
Delayed	Försenat
On time	I tid

1) When saying *"Tur & Retur"* (Round trip) you don't need to say *"biljett"* (ticket) as well since it is implicit.

Exercises/Övningar!

Translate (#2):

Swedish	English translation
- God morgon, hur kan jag hjälpa dig?	
- När avgår nästa tåg till Stockholm?	
- Det avgår klockan åtta på morgonen.	
- Tack. Jag skulle vilja ha en tur & retur till Stockholm.	
- Okej.	
- Vilken platform avgår tåget från?	

- Från platform tretton.	
- Okej, tack så mycket.	
- Varsågod, ha en trevlig resa.	

Translate (#3):

English	Swedish translation
- Hello, do you know when the train from Gothenburg arrives?	
- It's delayed but should be in around 6 p.m.	
- Okay, is there a waiting room close by?	
- It's over there to the left.	
- Thank you very much, goodbye.	

Chapter 11: Part 1 Answers

Fill in the blank with the word from the word bank:

1. I vilken <u>terminal</u> ligger gate 14?

2. Nu ska jag hämta min <u>resväska</u> i <u>bagageutlämningen</u>.

3. När jag hämtat väskan måste jag gå igenom <u>tullen</u>.

4. Hur mycket kostade din <u>biljett</u> till England?

5. Jag ska till Sverige med SAS <u>Flight 312</u> klockan 7.

Match the Vocabulary:

Swedish		English	
6. Flygplan	c.	Airplane	
7. Ha en trevlig resa.	d.	Have a nice trip.	
8. Biljett	b	Ticket	
9. Flygbolag	a.	Airline	

Translation:

Swedish	English translation
- Hej, hur kan jag hjälpa till?	- Hi, ma'am, how can I help you?
- Hej, när avgår flyget till Buenos Aires?	- Hi, when does the flight to Buenos Aires leave?
- Det avgår kl. 15.00.	- It takes off at 3:00 pm.
- Vilken gate avgår det från?	- What gate does it leave from?
- Från gate tio i terminal två.	- From gate 10 in terminal 2.
- Okej, tack så mycket.	- Okay, thank you sir.
- Varsågod, trevlig resa!	- Your welcome, bon voyage!

Chapter 11: Part 2 Answers

Match the Phrases:

Swedish		English
1. Du kan stanna här	c.	You can stop here
2. Sväng vänster vid rödljuset	e.	At the stoplight, turn left.
3. Hur mycket är jag skyldig?	b.	How much do I owe you?
4. Vart ska vi?	d.	Where are we going?
5. Här till höger.	a.	Here on the right.

Translation #1:

English	Swedish translation
- I'm going to Malmö, how much is it?	- Jag skall till Malmö, hur mycket kostar det?
- It's around SEK 300-.	- Det kostar ungefär 300 kronor.
- Okay, let's go.	- Okej, då åker vi.
- Where in Malmö do you want to go?	- Vart i Malmö vill du åka?
- To the train station please.	- Till tågstationen tack.
- Turn left here.	- Sväng vänster här.
- Okay, here it is.	- Okej, här är det.
- Thank you. Here you have 350 kronor, keep the change.	- Tack. Här har du 350 kr, behåll växeln.
- Thank you very much, goodbye ma'am.	- Tack så mycket, hej då.

Translation #2:

Swedish	English translation
- God morgon, hur kan jag hjälpa dig?	- Good morning, how can I help you?
- När avgår nästa tåg till Stockholm?	- What time does the next train leave for Stockholm?
- Det avgår klockan åtta på morgonen.	- It leaves at 8 in the morning.
- Tack. Jag skulle vilja ha en tur & retur till Stockholm.	- Thank you. I would like a round trip ticket to Stockholm.
- Okej.	- Okay.
- Vilken platform avgår tåget från?	- Which platform does the train leave from?

- Från platform tretton.	- From platform 13.
- Okej, tack så mycket.	- Okay, thank you very much.
- Varsågod, ha en trevlig resa.	- Your welcome, have a good trip.

Translation #3:

English	Swedish translation
- Hello, do you know when the train from Gothenburg arrives? - It's delayed but should be in around 6 p.m. - Okay, is there a waiting room close by? - It's over there to the left. - Thank you very much, goodbye.	- Hej, vet du när tåget från Göteborg ankommer? - Det är försenat men det borde ankomma ungefär 18.00. - Okej, finns det någon väntsal i närhet? - Den ligger där borta till vänster. - Tack så mycket, hej då.

Jag skulle vilja boka ett rum

Now that we have hopefully gotten you to your destination safe and sound without having gotten lost too many times, it is time to look for a place to stay. Whether you decide to stay in a hotel, hostal, or bed and breakfast, this chapter should help you through every step of the way. The standard of buildings in Sweden is usually the same or better than in the U.K., e.g. 3-glass windows were early adopted as standard due to the cold climate and in the kitchen and bathrooms you always have blenders instead of separate cold/hot water taps. Below, I have listed useful vocabulary and phrases for booking a room at your new destination. Enjoy your stay!

Hotel Vocabulary

English	Swedish
I would like to reserve a room for two people.	Jag skulle vilja reservera ett rum för två personer.
How much does it cost per night?	Hur mycket kostar det per natt?
For how many people?	För hur många personer?
For how many nights?	För hur många nätter?
For one night/two nights	För en kväll/två kvällar
With a double bed.	Med en dubbelsäng.
With two single beds	Med två enkelsängar.
I'm sorry, we are full.	Jag är ledsen, vi har fullt.
I have a reservation.	Jag har en reservation./Jag har en bokning.
Do you have wi-fi?	Har ni wi-fi?

Exercises/Övningar!

Match the Phrases:

English	↓	Swedish
1. I'm sorry we are full.		a. För hur många personer?
2. For how many people?		b. Jag är ledsen, vi har fullt.
3. I have a reservation.		c. För hur många nätter?
4. For how many nights?		d. Hur mycket kostar det per natt?

5. How much is it per night?			e. Jag har en bokning.

Translate to English:

Swedish	English translation
- Godkväll.	
- Godkväll, hur kan jag hjälpa er?	
- Jag skulle vilja boka ett rum för en person.	
- För hur många nätter?	
- För tre nätter.	
- Okej.	
- Hur mycket kostar det per natt?	
- Åttahundra kronor per natt.	
- Har ni wi-fi?	
- Ja, vi har wi-fi.	
- Tack så mycket.	

Chapter 12 Answers

Match the Phrases:

English		Swedish
1. I'm sorry we are full.	b.	Jag är ledsen, vi har fullt.
2. For how many people?	a.	För hur många personer?
3. I have a reservation.	e.	Jag har en bokning.
4. For how many nights?	c.	För hur många nätter?
5. How much is it per night?	d.	Hur mycket kostar det per natt?

Translation:

Swedish	English translation
- Godkväll.	- Good evening.
- Godkväll, hur kan jag hjälpa er?	- Good evening, how can I help you?
- Jag skulle vilja boka ett rum för en person.	- I would like to reserve a room for one person.
	- For how many nights?
- För hur många nätter?	- For three nights
- För tre nätter.	- Okay.
- Okej.	- How much is it per night?
- Hur mycket kostar det per natt?	- 800 kronor per night.
- Åttahundra kronor per natt.	- Do you have wi-fi?
- Har ni wi-fi?	- Yes, we have wi-fi.
- Ja, vi har wi-fi.	- Thank you very much.
- Tack så mycket.	

SECTION 3
GETTING TO KNOW EACH OTHER

Hur är…?

Now that we have gotten you through the essentials of getting around, finding a place to stay, and all of the other basics, we can focus on having a conversation in order to get to know people, make friends, etc. By the end of this section you will be able to talk about yourself, your family, work, and hobbies. The first chapter of this section is focused on description- how to describe yourself, other people, and things to others. Below, I have listed some useful vocabulary and phrases to help you describe the world around you.

Description Vocabulary

English	Swedish
tall / long	lång
short	kort
fat	fet
thin	small
pretty	vacker
handsome	stilig
cute	söt
hair	hår
big	stor
small	liten
strong	stark
ugly	ful
old	gammal
young	ung

Description Phrases and More Vocabulary

English	Swedish
What's it like?	Hur är det/den?
What does he/she look like?	Hur ser han/hon ut?
He is…/She is …	Han/Hon är …
I am…	Jag är…
What color is his/her hair?	Vilken färg har hans/hennes hår?

His/her hair is....	Hans/Hennes hår är...
Does she have long hair?	Har hon långt hår?
He has short hair.	Han har kort hår.
blonde	blond
brunette	brunett
red headed	rödhårig

Emotion Vocabulary

English	Swedish
How do you feel?	Hur mår du?
I feel good.	Jag mår bra.
I am happy.	Jag är glad.
Sad	Sad
Tired	Trött
Excited	Upphetsad
Bored	Uttråkad
Angry	Arg
Nervous	Nervös
Calm	Lugn
Busy	Upptagen
Scared	Rädd

Exercises/Övningar!

Translate to English:

Swedish	English translation
- Jag är lång och smal.	
- Hon är kort och söt.	
- Är han mycket gammal?	
- Vi är mycket stiliga.	
- De är starka.	

- Jag är mycket ledsen.	
- Hon är glad idag.	

Translate to Swedish:

English	Swedish translation
- What is she like?	
- She is tall, young and pretty.	
- What color is his/her hair?	
- She has long and blonde hair.	
- Does he have short hair?	
- Yes, he has short, black hair.	
- Is he nervous?	
- We are calm.	
- They are scared.	

Match the Vocabulary:

English	↓		Swedish
1. happy			a. uttråkad
2. Excited			b. ledsen
3. Nervous			c. glad
4. Bored			d. trött
5. Angry			e. upphetsad
6. Sad			f. rädd
7. Calm			g. nervös
8. Busy			h. arg
9. Scared			i. lugn

| 10. Tired | | | j. upptagen |

Chapter 13 Answers

Translation to English:

Swedish	English translation
- Jag är lång och smal.	- I am very tall and thin.
- Hon är kort och söt.	- She is short and cute.
- Är han mycket gammal?	- Is he very old?
- Vi är mycket stiliga.	- We are very handsome.
- De är starka.	- They are strong.
- Jag är mycket ledsen.	- I am very sad.
- Hon är glad idag.	- She is happy today.

Translation to Swedish:

English	Swedish translation
- What is she like?	- Hur är hon?
- She is tall, young and pretty.	- Hon är lång, ung och vacker.
- What color is his/her hair?	- Vilken färg har hans/hennes hår?
- She has long and blonde hair.	- Hon har långt och blont hår.
- Does he have short hair?	- Har han kort hår?
- Yes, he has short, black hair.	- Ja, han hark ort, svart hår.
- Is he nervous?	- Är han nervös?
- We are calm.	- Vi är lugna.
- They are scared.	- De är rädda.

Match the Vocabulary:

English		Swedish
1. happy	c.	glad
2. Excited	e.	upphetsad
3. Nervous	g.	nervös
4. Bored	a.	uttråkad
5. Angry	h.	arg
6. Sad	b.	ledsen
7. Calm	i.	lugn
8. Busy	j.	upptagen
9. Scared	f.	rädd
10. Tired	d.	trött

Jag är gift och har två barn

In this chapter you will be able to talk about your family – how many brothers and sisters you have, are they older or younger, etc. You will also be able to talk about your more extended family- aunts, uncles, cousins, grandparents, etc. Below you will learn useful language to describe your family.

Family vocabulary and phrases

English	Swedish
How many siblings do you have?	Hur många syskon har du?
I have 3 siblings.	Jag har tre syskon.
Brother	Bror
Sister	Syster
Mother/Mom	Mamma
Father/Dad	Pappa
Grandpa (on fathers side)	Farfar
Grandpa (on mothers side)	Morfar
Grandma (on fathers side)	Farmor
Grandma (on mothers side)	Mormor
Cousin	Kusin
Husband	Man/Make
Wife	Hustru/Maka
Son/Daughter	Son/Dotter
Uncle/Aunt (on fathers side)	Farbror/Faster
Uncle/Aunt (on mothers side)	Morbror/Moster
Pet	Sällskapsdjur
Dog	Hund
Cat	Katt
Older	Äldre
Younger	Yngre

It's useful to know the possessive pronouns in order to talk about family, so you can say – *my* mom, *his* sister, *her* grandma, etc.

Possessive Pronouns

English	Swedish
My	Min
Your	Din
His/Hers	Hans/Hennes
Our	Vår
Their	Deras

Exercises/Övningar!

Translate to English:

Swedish	English translation
- Jag har tre bröder.	
- Han har tio kusiner.	
- Har hon många syskon?	
- Vi har två barn.	
- Dom har en hund och en katt.	

Match the Vocabulary:

Swedish	↓		English
1. Make			a. Older
2. Fru			b. Dad
3. Morbror			c. Husband
4. Faster			d. Younger
5. Äldre			e. Wife
6. Yngre			f. Grandma
7. Make			g. Aunt
8. Morfar			h. Uncle
9. Farmor			i. Cousine
10. Pappa			j. Grandpa

Put the possessive pronouns in the correct form;

English	Swedish
1. <u>My</u> brothers are very tall.	_____ bröder är mycket långa.
2. <u>His</u> sister is cute.	_____ syster är söt.
3. <u>Our</u> grandma is very nice.	_____ mormor är mycket trevlig.
4. <u>Your</u> father is rather short	_____ pappa är ganska kort.
5. <u>Their</u> sons are very young.	_____ söner är mycket unga.

Write about your family following the example:

Jag har en fru och två döttrar. Jag har även en äldre bror. Hans namn är Peter och han är trettiotre år gammal. Han har en vacker fru som heter Eva. Jag gillar verkligen min mormor.

Chapter 14 Answers

Translation to English:

Swedish	English translation
- Jag har tre bröder.	- I have three brothers.
- Han har tio kusiner.	- He has ten cousins.
- Har hon många syskon?	- Does she have many siblings?
- Vi har två barn.	- We have two children.
- Dom har en hund och en katt.	- They have a dog and a cat.

Match the Vocabulary:

Swedish		English	
1. Kusin	i.	Cousine
2. Fru	e.	Wife
3. Morbror	h.	Uncle
4. Faster	g.	Aunt
5. Äldre	a.	Older
6. Yngre	d.	Younger
7. Make	c.	Husband
8. Morfar	j.	Grandpa
9. Farmor	f.	Grandma
10. Pappa	b.	Dad

Put the possessive pronouns in the correct form;

English	Swedish
1. My brothers are very tall.	Mina bröder är mycket långa.
2. His sister is cute.	Hans syster är söt.
3. Our grandma is very nice.	Vår mormor är mycket trevlig.
4. Your father is rather short	Din pappa är ganska kort.
5. Their sons are very young.	Deras söner är mycket unga.

Writing about your family following the example

Swedish:

Jag har en fru och två döttrar. Jag har även en äldre bror. Hans namn är Peter och han är trettiotre år gammal. Han har en vacker fru som heter Eva. Jag gillar verkligen min mormor.

English translation:

I have a wife and two daughters. I also have an older brother. His name is Peter and he is 33 ears old. He has a very pretty wife named Eva. I really like my grandmother.

Vad jobbar du med?

Now that we are able to describe ourselves physically and discuss our family, we can talk about what we do, our career. It is something that we often talk about and sometimes unfortunately can consume our lives. In Sweden work is a big part of life. For many people much is centered around making a career, often at the expense of family and friends. In this chapter, you will learn some basic professions of our society.

Occupational vocabulary and phrases

English	Swedish
What do you do?	Vad arbetar/jobbar du med? [1]
I am a teacher.	Jag är lärare/lärarinna (male/female)
businessman/business woman	affärsman/affärskvinna
cleaner	lokalvårdare
doctor	doktor
nurse	sjuksköterska [2]
attorney	advokat
lawyer	advokat/jurist
writer	författare
policeman	polis
firefighter	brandman
student	student
receptionist	receptionist
waiter	servitor/servitris (male/female)
cook	kock
salesperson	säljare
engineer	ingenjör
employer	arbetsgivare
employee	anställd/arbetstagare

1) "Working" can be said in two ways, "*arbetar*" and "*jobbar*". Both are equivalent.
2) Today it is the same for both male and female.

Exercises/Övningar!

Match the Vocabulary:

Swedish	↓	English
1. advokat		a. police officer
2. kock		b. nurse
3. servitör		c. doctor
4. polis		d. businessman
5. sjuksköterska		e. salesperson
6. affärsman		f. waiter
7. doktor		g. firefighter
8. ingenjör		h. attorney
9. säljare		i. engineer
10. brandman		j. cook

Translate to Swedish:

English	Swedish translation
- She is an excellent lawyer.	
- They are firefighters.	
- My sister works as a receptionist.	
- They are both writers.	
- He is my employer.	

Chapter 15 Answers

Match the Vocabulary:

Swedish		English
1. advokat	h.	attorney
2. kock	i.	engineer
3. servitör	f.	waiter
4. polis	a.	police officer
5. sjuksköterska	b.	nurse
6. affärsman	d.	businessman
7. doktor	c.	doctor
8. ingenjör	j.	cook
9. säljare	e.	salesperson
10. brandman	g.	firefighter

Translation to Swedish:

English	Swedish translation
- She is an excellent lawyer.	- Hon är en utmärkt jurist.
- They are firefighters.	- De är brandmän.
- My sister works as a receptionist.	- Min syster arbetar som receptionist.
- They are both writers.	- De är båda författare.
- He is my employer.	- Han är min arbetsgivare.

Gillar du att...?

Now that we have learned how to describe yourself, your family, and occupation, we can move onto discussing what you enjoy doing in your free time.

Contrary to Latin American countries with a cultural where they often spend their free time with family they in Sweden more often look for own individual hobbies and interests and try to spend most of our free time with our friends, away from family. A very large part of the population engages in physical activities in their free time since fitness and well-being have a high priority. Below you will find useful phrases to discuss hobbies so that you can talk about what you like.

Vocabulary to discuss your Hobbies

English	Swedish
Hobby	Hobby/Fritidsintresse
What do you like to do?	Vad tycker du om att göra?
I like ...	Jag tycker om att ... / Jag gillar att ...
I don't like	Jag tycker inte om att... / Jag gillar inte att...
free time	fritid
sport / play sports	sport / sporta
play videogames	spela videospel
travel	resa
read	läsa
go to the movies	gå på bio
go to the beach	vara på stranden
watch TV	se på TV
watch sports	se på sport
listen to music	lyssna på musik
play instruments	spela instrument
dance	dans
exercise	motion
swim	simma
cycling	cykla
jog/run	jogga/springa

ski	åka skidor
spend time with friends	vara med vänner
evenings at home	hemmakvällar
romantic dinner	romantiska middar

- Words like work-out, aerobics, golf, spinning, jet-ski etc are taken directly from English so they are the same.
- You will learn how to conjugate regular verbs in the last section of this book.

Exercises/Övningar!

Choose the correct answer:

1. I like to go to the movies. _____

a. Jag tycker om att vara på stranden.	b. Jag gillar att gå till stranden.
c. Jag tycker om att lyssna på musik.	d. Jag tycker om att gå på bio.

2. Do you like to read? _____

a. Tycker du om att resa?	b. Du liknar en råtta.
c. Tycker du om att läsa?	d. Tycker du om motion?

3. I don't like to travel. _____

a. Jag tycker om att resa.	b. Jag gillar inte att resa.
c. Jag tycker inte om tavlan.	d. Jag tycker inte om att dansa.

Match the Phrases:

Swedish	↓	English	
1. Vill du åka skidor?		a. Spend time with friends.	
2. Vara med vänner.		b. Do you want to go to the beach?	
3. Gillar du att motionera?		c. I like to travel.	
4. Vill du gå till stranden?		d. Do you want to ski?	
5. Jag tycker om att resa.		e. Do you like to exercise?	

Chapter 16 Answers

Choose the correct answer:

1. I like to go to the movies.	d. Jag tycker om att gå på bio.
2. Do you like to read?	c. Tycker du om att läsa?
3. I don't like to travel.	b. Jag gillar inte att resa.

Match the Phrases:

Swedish		English
1. Vill du åka skidor?	d.	Do you want to ski?
2. Vara med vänner.	a.	Spend time with friends.
3. Gillar du att motionera?	e.	Do you like to exercise?
4. Vill du gå till stranden?	b.	Do you want to go to the beach?
5. Jag tycker om att resa.	c.	I like to travel.

SECTION 4: GRAMMAR SCHOOL

Grammar Topics for Swedish Learners

Chapter 17: Nouns

Swedish belongs to the Indo-European family, Germanic group, Scandinavian subgroup and is spoken by 9 million people. Swedish is closely related to the other Scandinavian languages and somewhat less close to German, Dutch and English. Historically it is closer to Danish, but the years of Swedish hegemony over Norway (1814-1905) brought the two languages closer together. During the Middle Ages Swedish borrowed many words from German, while the 18th century witnessed a large infusion of words from the Swedish. In the 19th and 20th centuries English has become by far the largest source of foreign borrowings. The English words "smorgasbord" and "tungsten" are of Swedish origin. The former is a combination of "smörgås" (sandwich) and "bord" (table), the latter is a combination of "tung" (heavy) and "sten" (stone). There are at least four Swedish dialects with the same "high" status, but the one spoken in Svealand is considered to be "proper" Swedish.

Nouns have two grammatical genders: common (utrum) and neuter (neutrum), which determine their definite forms as well as the form of any adjectives used to describe them. Noun gender is largely arbitrary and must be memorized; however, around three quarters of all Swedish nouns are common gender. Living beings are often common nouns, like inen katt, en häst, en fluga, etc.

Swedish nouns are inflected for number and definiteness and can take a genitive suffix. They exhibit the following morpheme order:

Noun stem	(Plural)	(Definite article)	(Genitive -s)

Plural forms

Nouns form the plural in a variety of ways. It is customary to classify regular Swedish nouns into five declensions based on their plural indefinite endings: -or, -ar, -er, -n, and unchanging nouns.

All nouns of common gender ending in _-a_ replace this ending with _–or_.
Example: _flicka_ (girl), _flickor_ (girls).

There are also a few other words with plurals in _–or_.

Examples: *våg* (wave), *vågor* (waves); toffel (slipper), *tofflor* (slippers); *ros* (rose), *rosor* (roses).

Note however that *toffel* is interchangeable with *toffla*, in which case the plural tofflor would not be irregular at all.

Most nouns of common gender not ending in **_a_** add either **-_ar_**, **-_er_**, or (rarely) **-_r_**.
While **-_ar_** is slightly more common, there is no reliable rule to determine which suffix to use.

Examples: *växt* (plant), *växter* (plants); *lök* (onion), *lökar* (onions).
All neuter nouns ending in a vowel add **-_n_**.

Example: *äpple* (apple), *äpplen* (apples).
Except for: *öga* (eye), *ögon* (eyes) and *öra* (ear), *öron* (ears).

All neuter nouns ending in a consonant are unchanged in the plural.
Example: *barn* (child) or *barn* (children).

There are also some irregular nouns—their number is not great, but they are some of the most commonly used nouns.

Mildly irregular nouns are common nouns that are unchanged in the plural, nouns that double a consonant and shorten a vowel in the plural, etc.
Example: *gås* (goose), *gäss* (geese).

As allway – there are exceptions.

Articles and definite forms

The definite article in Swedish is mostly expressed by a suffix on the head noun, while the indefinite article is a separate word preceding the noun. This structure of the articles is shared by the Scandinavian languages. Articles differ in form depending on the gender and number of the noun.

The indefinite article, which is only used in the singular, is "**_en_**" for common nouns, and "**_ett_**" for neuter nouns.
Examples: *en flaska* (a bottle), *ett brev* (a letter).

The definite article in the singular is generally the suffixes *-en* or *-n* for common nouns and *-et* or *-t* for neuter nouns.
Examples: *flaskan* (the bottle), *brevet* (the letter).

The definite article in the plural is *-na*, *-a* or *-en*, depending on declension group, for example *flaskorna* (the bottles), *breven* (the letters).

When an adjective or numeral is used in front of a noun with the definite article, an additional definite article is placed before the adjective(s). This additional definite article is *det* for neuter nouns, *den* for common nouns, and *de* for plural nouns.
Examples: *den nya flaskan* (the new bottle), *det nya brevet* (the new letter), *de fem flaskorna* (the five bottles).

A similar structure involving the same kind of circumfixing of the definite article with the words *där* (there) or *här* (here) is used to mean "this" and "that" as a demonstrative article.
Examples: *den här flaskan* (this bottle), *det där brevet* (that letter).
The five declension classes may be named -or, -ar, -er, -n, and null after their respective plural indefinite endings. Each noun has eight forms: singular/plural, definite/indefinite and caseless/genitive. The caseless form is sometimes referred to as nominative, even though it is used for grammatical objects as well as subjects.

The genitive

The genitive is always formed by appending *-s* to the caseless form. In the second, third and fifth declensions words may end with an *-s* already in the caseless form. These words take no extra *-s* in genitive use, like the genitive (indefinite) of *hus* ("house") is *hus.*

Examples

These examples cover all regular Swedish caseless noun forms.

First declension: *-or* (common gender).

	Singular	Plural
Indefinite	*(en) flaska* (a) bottle	*flaskor* bottles
Definite	*flaskan*	*flaskorna*

	the bottle	the bottles

Second declension: -ar (common gender).

	Singular	Plural
Indefinite	*(en) stol* a chair	*stolar* chairs
Definite	*stolen* the chair	*stolarna* the chairs

	Singular	Plural
Indefinite	*(en) gubbe* (an) old man	*gubbar* old men
Definite	*gubben* the old man	*gubbarna* the old men

Third declension: -er, -r (mostly common gender nouns, some neuter nouns).

	Singular	Plural
Indefinite	*(en) sak* (a) thing	*saker* things
Definite	*saken* the thing	*sakerna* the things

	Singular	Plural
Indefinite	*(en) bakelse* (a) pastry	*bakelser* pastries
Definite	*bakelsen* the pastry	*bakelserna* the pastries

	Singular	Plural
Indefinite	*(ett) parti* (a) political party	*partier* political parties
Definite	*partiet* the political party	*partierna* the political parties

Fourth declension: -n (neuter) This is when a neuter noun ends in a vowel.

	Singular	Plural
Indefinite	*(ett) hjärta* (a) heart	*hjärtan* hearts
Definite	*hjärtat* the heart	*hjärtana* the hearts

Fifth declension: unmarked plural (mostly neuter nouns that don't end in vowels and common gender nouns ending in certain derivation suffixes).

	Singular	Plural

	Singular	Plural

Indefinite	(en) bagare (a) baker	bagare bakers
Definite	bagaren the baker	bagarna the bakers

Indefinite	(en) indier (an) Indian	indier Indians
Definite	indiern the Indian	indierna the Indians

	Singular	Plural
Indefinite	(ett) horn (a) horn	horn horns
Definite	hornet the horn	hornen the horns

Exercises/Övningar!

Translate to Swedish, with the nouns in correct form:

English	Swedish translation
Both my thumbs hurts but right thumb does hurt the most. The thumbs are probably ok tomorrow. Can you put a patch on this thumb?	
I have many books, but this book is the best. Please, put my book among those other books.	
She is just a child among many other children. That child is smallest the smallest of all the children.	
Those easels are white but my easel is black. Almost all easels are intact but this easel is broken.	
This one is just one bar among many other bars, but this bar is better than all the other bars.	

We have to <u>cars</u>. One of the <u>cars</u> is new. That <u>car</u> is rather small. My son has no <u>car</u>.	
Look, a <u>flea</u>! Actually, there are many <u>fleas</u>. Ignore those <u>fleas</u> but kill that <u>flea</u>.	
My quilt is so hot so I don't need more <u>quilts</u>. Put thos two <u>quilts</u> in the wardrobe. The <u>quilt</u> needs to be washed.	

Chapter 17 Answers

Translation to Swedish:

English	Swedish translation
Both my <u>thumbs</u> hurts but right <u>thumb</u> does hurt the most. The <u>thumbs</u> are probably ok tomorrow. Can you put a patch on this <u>thumb</u>?	Båda mina <u>tummar</u> gör ont men höger <u>tumme</u> gör ondast. <u>Tummarna</u> är nog ok imorgon. Kan du sätta ett plåster på denna <u>tummen</u>?
I have many <u>books</u>, but this <u>book</u> is the best. Please, put my <u>book</u> among those other <u>books</u>.	Jag har många <u>böcker</u> men den här <u>boken</u> är bäst. Snälla, ställ min <u>bok</u> bland dom där andra <u>böckerna</u>.
She is just a <u>child</u> among many other <u>children</u>. That <u>child</u> is smallest the smallest of all the <u>children</u>.	Hon är bara ett <u>barn</u> bland många andra <u>barn</u>. Det <u>barnet</u> är det minsta av alla <u>barnen</u>.
Those <u>easels</u> are white but my <u>easel</u> is black. Almost all <u>easels</u> are intact but this <u>easel</u> is broken.	De <u>stafflierna</u> är vita men mitt <u>staffli</u> i svart. Nästan alla <u>stafflier</u> är hela men det <u>staffliet</u> är trasigt.
This one is just one <u>bar</u> among many other <u>bars</u>, but this <u>bar</u> is better than all the other <u>bars</u>.	Den här är bara en <u>bar</u> bland många andra <u>barer</u>, men den här <u>baren</u> är bättre än alla de andra <u>barerna</u>.
We have to <u>cars</u>. One of the <u>cars</u> is new. That <u>car</u> is rather small. My son has no <u>car</u>.	Vi har två blå <u>bilar</u>. En av <u>bilarna</u> är ny. Den <u>bilen</u> är ganska liten. Min son har ingen <u>bil</u>.
Look, a <u>flea</u>! Actually, there are many <u>fleas</u>. Ignore those <u>fleas</u> but kill that <u>flea</u>.	Titta, en <u>loppa</u>! Där är faktiskt många <u>loppor</u>. Ignorera dom (de) <u>lopporna</u> men döda den <u>loppan</u>.
My quilt is so hot so I don't need more <u>quilts</u>. Put thos two <u>quilts</u> in the wardrobe. The <u>quilt</u> needs to be washed.	Mitt <u>täcke</u> är så varmt så jag behöver inte fler <u>täcken</u>. Lägg dom två <u>täckena</u> i skåpet. <u>Täcket</u> behöver tvättas.

The Swedish personal pronoun system is almost identical to that of English. Pronouns inflect for person, number, and, in the third person singular, gender. Differences with English include the inclusion in Swedish of a separate third-person reflexive pronoun sig (himself, herself, itself, themselves) analogous to French "se", and the maintenance of distinct 2nd person singular *du* ("thou"), *ni* (you) plural, and objective forms of those, which have all merged to "you" in English, while the third person plurals are becoming merged in Swedish instead.

Some aspects of personal pronouns are simpler in Swedish: reflexive forms are not used for the first and second person, although **själv** (self) and **egen/eget/egna** (own) may be used for emphasis, and there are no absolute forms for the possessive.

The Swedish personal pronouns are:

Singular				
Person	**Eng.**	**Nominative**	**Objective**	**Possessive: com./neut./pl.**
1	I	*jag*	*mig*	*min/mitt/mina*[1]
2 (familiar)	you	*du*	*dig*	*din/ditt/dina*[1]
3 Masc.	he	*han*	*honom*	*hans*
3 Fem.	she	*hon*	*henne*	*hennes*
3 Gen-Neu.	he/she	*hen*[4]	*henom*[4]	*hens*[4]
3 Com.	it	*den*	*den*	*dess*
3 Neu.	it	*det*	*det*	*dess*
3 Indef.	"one"	*man* ("one", Fr. "on")	*en*	*ens*
(3 Refl.)	-	—	*sig*	*sin/sitt/sina*[1]

Plural

Person	(Eng.)	Nominative	Objective	Possessive: com./neut./pl.
1	we	*vi*	*oss*	*vår/vårt/våra*[1]
2 (formal: sg. or pl.)	you	*ni*[3]	*er*	*er/ert/era*[1], *Ers* (honorific)
3	they	*de*[2]	*dem*[2]	*deras*
(3 Refl.)	-	—	*sig*	*sin/sitt/sina*[1]

1) These possessive pronouns are inflected similarly to adjectives, agreeing in gender and number with the item possessed. The other possessive pronouns (i.e. those listed without slashes) are genitive forms that are unaffected by the item possessed.

2) de (they) and dem (them) are both usually pronounced "dom" (/dɔm/) in colloquial speech, while in proper speech, "dom" may optionally replace just "dem". In some dialects (especially in Finnish ones) there is still a separation between the two, de is then commonly pronounced /di/. Note also that mig, dig, sig are pronounced as if written "mej", "dej", "sej", and are also sometimes spelled that way in less formal writing or to signal spoken language, but this is not appreciated by everyone.

3) ni is derived from an older pronoun I, "ye", for which verbs were always conjugated with the ending -en. I became ni when this conjugation was dropped; thus the n was moved from the end of the verb to the beginning of the pronoun.

4) hen and its inflections are gender-neutral pronouns used to avoid a preference for female or male, when a person's gender is not known, or to refer to people whose gender is not defined as female or male. It is relatively new in widespread use, but since 2010 has appeared frequently in traditional and online media,[4] legal documents,[5] and literature.

Demonstrative, interrogative, and relative pronouns

including related words not strictly considered pronouns

- ***den här, det här, de här***: this, these (may qualify a noun in the definite form).
- ***den där, det där, de där***: that, those (may qualify a noun in the definite form).
- ***denne/denna/detta/dessa***: this/these (may qualify a noun in the indefinite form).

- **som**: as, that, which, who (strictly speaking, a subordinating conjunction rather than a pronoun, som is used as an all-purpose relative pronoun whenever possible in Swedish).
- **vem**: who, whom (interrogative).
- **vilken, vilket, vilka**: which, what, who, whom, that.
- **vad**: what.
- **vems**: whose (interrogative).
- **vars**: whose (relative).
- **när**: when.
- **då**[1]: then, when (relative).
- **här, där, var**[1]: here, there, where (also form numerous combinations such as **varifrån**, "where from", and **därav**, "thereof").
- **hit, dit, vart**[1]: hither, thither, whither (not archaic as in English).
- **vem som helst, vilket som helst, vad som helst, när som helst, var som helst**: whoever, whichever, whatever, whenever, wherever, etc.
- **hädan, dädan, vadan, sedan**[1]: hence, thence, whence, since (The contractions **hän** and **sen** are common. These are all somewhat archaic and formal-sounding except **för sedan**.).
- **någon, något, några**, often contracted to and nearly always said as *nån/nåt/nåra*[2]: some/any, a few; someone/anyone, somebody/anybody, something/anything. (The distinction between "some" in an affirmative statement and "any" in a negative or interrogative context is actually a slight difficulty for Swedes learning English).
- **ingen/inget/inga**[2]: no, none; no one, nobody, nothing.
- **annan/annat/andra**: other, else.
- **någonstans, ingenstans, annanstans, överallt**: somewhere/anywhere, nowhere, elsewhere, everywhere; (more formally *någonstädes, ingenstädes, annorstädes, allestädes*).
- **någorlunda, ingalunda, annorlunda**: somehow/anyhow, in no wise, otherwise.
- **någonting, ingenting, allting**: something/anything, nothing, everything.

1) **då, där, dit**, and <u>dädan</u>, (then, there, thither, and thence,) and any compounds derived from them are used not only in a demonstrative sense, but also in a relative sense, where English would require the "wh-" forms when, where, whither and whence.

2) Animacy is implied by gender in these pronouns: non-neuter implies a person (-one or -body) and neuter implies a thing.

Exercises/Övningar!

Translate to Swedish, using the correct <u>personal</u> pronouns:

English	Swedish translation
I gave the book to <u>you</u> instead of <u>him</u>.	
Give <u>it</u> back to <u>me</u> after <u>you</u> read <u>it</u>.	
Do <u>you</u> want <u>my</u> apples or <u>my</u> pear?	
<u>She</u> looked at <u>him</u> and <u>he</u> looked back at <u>her</u>.	
<u>That</u> stone is heavy and <u>its</u> color is black.	
<u>That</u> table is made by oak. <u>Its</u> color is brown.	
<u>His</u> watch was nice. <u>He</u> gave <u>it</u> to me.	
<u>We</u> wish <u>you</u> all a Merry Christmas!	
<u>My</u> gift to <u>you</u> all is secret.	
Later <u>I</u> gave <u>them</u> expensive gifts for <u>their</u> good work.	
<u>Our</u> effort is only for <u>your</u> own best.	

Translate to Swedish, using the correct <u>non-personal</u> pronouns:

English	Swedish translation
<u>This</u> vase is beautiful.	
Can you put <u>something</u> here, <u>no one</u> else will do it.	

When can you pick up <u>some</u> onions? <u>Whenever</u> it suits you.	
<u>What</u> are you thinking? <u>Nothing</u> that concerns you!	
<u>Whoever</u> can try but <u>no one</u> can beat me.	

Chapter 18 Answers

Translation to Swedish, (with <u>personal</u> pronouns):

English	Swedish translation
<u>I</u> gave the book to <u>you</u> instead of <u>him</u>.	<u>Jag</u> gav boken till <u>dig</u> istället för <u>honom</u>.
Give <u>it</u> back to <u>me</u> after <u>you</u> read <u>it</u>.	Ge tillbaka <u>den</u> till <u>mig</u> efter <u>du</u> läst <u>den</u>.
Do <u>you</u> want <u>my</u> apples or <u>my</u> pear?	Vill <u>du</u> ha <u>mina</u> äpplen eller <u>mitt</u> päron.
<u>She</u> looked at <u>him</u> and <u>he</u> looked back at <u>her</u>.	<u>Hon</u> tittade på <u>honom</u> och <u>han</u> tittade tillbaka på <u>henne</u>.
<u>That</u> stone is heavy and <u>its</u> color is black.	<u>Den</u> stenen är tung och <u>dess</u> färg är svart.
<u>That</u> table is made by oak. <u>Its</u> color is brown.	<u>Det</u> bordet är gjort av ek. <u>Dess</u> färg är brun.
<u>His</u> watch was nice. <u>He</u> gave <u>it</u> to me.	<u>Hans</u> klocka var fin. <u>Han</u> gav <u>den</u> till <u>mig</u>.
<u>We</u> wish <u>you</u> all a Merry Christmas!	<u>Vi</u> önskar <u>er</u> alla en God Jul!
<u>My</u> gift to <u>you</u> all is secret.	<u>Min</u> present till <u>er</u> alla är hemlig.
Later <u>I</u> gave <u>them</u> expensive gifts for <u>their</u> good work.	Senare gav <u>jag</u> <u>dem</u> dyra presenter för <u>deras</u> bra arbete.
<u>Our</u> effort is only for <u>your</u> own best.	<u>Vår</u> ansträngning är bara för <u>ditt</u> eget bästa.

Translation to Swedish, (with non-<u>personal</u> pronouns):

English	Swedish translation
<u>This</u> vase is beautiful.	<u>Den här</u> vasen är vacker.
Can you put <u>something</u> here, <u>no one</u> else will do it.	Kan du ställa <u>något</u> här, <u>ingen annan</u> kommer att göra det.
When can you pick up <u>some</u> onions? <u>Whenever</u> it suits you.	När kan du plocka upp <u>några</u> lökar? <u>När som helst</u> det passar dig.
<u>What</u> are you thinking? <u>Nothing</u> that concerns you!	<u>Vad</u> tänker du på? <u>Inget/Ingenting</u> som berör dig!
<u>Whoever</u> can try but <u>no one</u> can beat me.	<u>Vem som helst</u> kan försöka men <u>ingen</u> kan slå mig.

Chapter 19: Adjectives

Swedish adjectives are declined according to gender, number, and definiteness of the noun.

Strong inflection

In singular indefinite, the form used with nouns of the common gender is the undeclined form, but with nouns of the neuter gender a suffix *-t* is added. In plural indefinite an *-a* suffix is added irrespective of gender. This constitutes the strong adjective inflection, characteristic of Germanic languages:

	Singular	Plural
Common	*en stor* björn, a large bear	*stora björnar*, large bears
Neuter	*ett stort* lodjur, a large lynx	*stora lodjur*, large lynxes

In standard Swedish, adjectives are inflected according to the strong pattern, by gender and number of the noun, in complement function with *är*, is, such as ...

lodjuret är skyggt, the lynx is shy, and
björnarna är bruna, the bears are brown.

Weak inflection

In definite form we instead have a weak adjective inflection, originating from a Proto-Germanic nominal derivation of the adjectives. The adjectives now invariably take on an *-a* suffix irrespective of case and number, which was not always the case, cf. Proto-Germanic adjectives:

	Singular	Plural
Common	den stora björnen, the large bear	de stora björnarna, the large bears
Neuter	det stora lodjuret, the large lynx	de stora lodjuren, the large lynxes

As the sole exception to this -a suffix is that naturally masculine nouns (replaceable with han/honom) take the -e ending in singular. Colloquially however the usual -a-ending is possible in these cases in some Sveamål dialects:

	Singular	Plural
Nat. masc., alt. I	den store mannen, the large man	de stora männen, the large men
Nat. masc., alt. II	den stora mannen, the large man	

Exercises/Övningar!

Translate to Swedish, with the adjectives in correct form:

English	Swedish translation
Here is a <u>yellow</u> lion. Over there are several <u>yellow</u> lions. My pen is also <u>yellow</u>.	
A <u>happy</u> girl kisses the <u>sad</u> boy.	
The flowers are <u>tall</u> and <u>fine</u> as they stand in a <u>warm</u> greenhouse.	
The <u>white</u> cloud is floating on the <u>blue</u> sky. It would be fun to see a <u>blue</u> cloud on a <u>white</u> sky.	

Chapter 19 Answers

Translation to Swedish:

English	Swedish translation
Here is a yellow lion. Over there are several yellow lions. My pen is also yellow.	Här är ett <u>gult</u> lejon. Där borta finns fler <u>gula</u> lejon. Min penna är också <u>gul</u>.
A <u>happy</u> girl kisses the <u>sad</u> boy.	En <u>glad</u> flicka pussar/kysser den ledsna pojken.
The flowers are <u>tall</u> and <u>fine</u> as they stand in a <u>warm</u> greenhouse.	Blommorna är <u>höga</u> och <u>fina</u> eftersom de står i ett <u>varmt</u> växthus.
The <u>white</u> cloud is floating on the <u>blue</u> sky. It would be fun to see a	Det <u>vita</u> molnet sväver på den <u>blå</u> himlen.

| blue cloud on a white sky. | Det skulle vara kul att se ett blått moln på en vit himmel. |

Adjectives with comparative and superlative forms ending in **-are** and **-ast**, which is a majority, also, and so by rule, use the **-e** suffix for all persons on definite superlatives.

Example: *den billigaste bilen* (the cheapest car).

Another instance of **-e** for all persons is the plural forms and definite forms of adjectival verb participles ending in **-ad**.

Example: *en målad bil* (a painted car) vs. *målade bilar* (painted cars) and *den målade bilen* ("the painted car").

Exercises/Övningar!

Translate to Swedish:

English	Swedish translation
This boat is expensive. Those over there are more expensive but that one is the most expensive.	
Those cups are polished but this cup is not polished.	
My girlfriend is sweet, not sweeter than Eva though. Eva is the sweetest in the world.	

Chapter 20 Answers

Translation to Swedish:

English	Swedish translation
This boat is expensive. Those over there are more	Den här båten är dyr. De där borta är dyrare men den där är dyrast.

<u>expensive</u> but that one is the <u>most expensive</u>.	
Those cups are <u>polished</u> but this cup is not <u>polished</u>.	De där kopparna är <u>putsade</u> men den här koppen är inte <u>putsad</u>.
My girlfriend is <u>sweet</u>, not <u>sweeter</u> than Eva though. Eva is the <u>sweetest</u> in the world.	Min flickvän är <u>söt</u>, inte <u>sötare</u> än Eva dock. Eva är den <u>sötaste</u> i världen.

Chapter 21: Numerals

Cardinal numbers

The cardinal numbers from zero to twelve in Swedish are:

0	1	2	3	4	5	6	7	8	9	10	11	12
noll	en/ett	två	tre	fyra	fem	sex	sju	åtta	nio	tio	elva	tolv

The number 1 is the same as the indefinite article, and its form (*en/ett*) depends on the gender of the noun that it modifies.

The Swedish numbers from 13 to 19 are:

13	14	15	16	17	18	19
tretton	fjorton	femton	sexton	sjutton	arton	nitton

The numbers for multiples of ten from 20 to 1000 are:

20	30	40	50	60	70	80	90	100	1000
tjugo	tretti o	fyrti o	femti o	sexti o	sjutti o	åtti o	nitti o	(ett) hundra	(ett) tusen

Higher numbers include:

10 000	tiotusen
100 000	hundratusen
1 000 000	en miljon
10 000 000	tio miljoner
100 000 000	(ett) hundra miljoner

1 000 000 000	en miljard 1)

1) Swedish uses the <u>long scale for large numbers</u>.

The cardinal numbers from *miljon* and larger are true nouns and take the -*er* suffix in the plural. They are separated in written Swedish from the preceding number.

	Written form	In components (do not use in written Swedish)
21	*tjugoett / tjugoen*	(tjugo-ett) / (tjugo-en)
147	*etthundrafyrtisju* *etthundrafyrtiosju*	(ett-hundra-fyrtio-sju)
1 975	*ettusen niohundrasjuttifem* *ettusen niohundrasjuttiofem*	(ett-tusen nio-hundra-sjuttio-fem)
10 874	*tiotusen åttahundrasjuttifyra* *tiotusen åttahundrasjuttiofyra*	(tio-tusen åtta-hundra-sjuttio-fyra)
100 557	*etthundratusen femhundrafemtisju* *etthundratusen femhundrafemtiosju*	(ett-hundra-tusen fem-hundra-femtio-sju)
1 378 971	*en miljon trehundrasjuttiåtta tusen niohundrasjuttiett* *en miljon trehundrasjuttioåtta tusen niohundrasjuttioett*	(en miljon tre-hundra-sjuttio-åtta tusen nio-hundra-sjuttio-ett)

The decimal point is written as "," (comma) and written and pronounced *komma*. When dealing with monetary amounts (usually with two decimals), the decimal point is read as *och*, i.e. "and".
Examples: 3,50 (*tre och femtio*), 7,88 (*sju och åttioåtta*).

Rational numbers are read as the cardinal number of the numerator followed by the ordinal number of the denominator compounded with *-del* or -*delar* (part(s)). If the numerator is more than one, logically, the plural form of *del* is used. For those ordinal numbers that are three syllables or longer and end in *-de*, that suffix is usually dropped in favour of the *de* in -*del*. There are a few exceptions.

$\frac{1}{2}$	*en halv*, (one half)		$\frac{1}{12}$	*en tolftedel*
$\frac{1}{3}$	*en tredjedel*		$\frac{1}{13}$	*en trettondel*
$\frac{3}{4}$	*tre fjärdedelar*		$\frac{1}{14}$	*en fjortondel*

$^2/_5$	två femtedelar	$^1/_{15}$	en femtondel
$^5/_6$	fem sjättedelar	$^1/_{16}$	en sextondel
$^4/_7$	fyra sjundedelar	$^1/_{17}$	en sjuttondel
$^1/_8$	en åttondel or en åttondedel	$^1/_{18}$	en artondel
$^8/_9$	åtta niondelar or åtta niondedelar	$^1/_{19}$	en nittondel
$^1/_{10}$	en tiondel or en tiondedel	$^1/_{20}$	en tjugonde
$^1/_{11}$	en elftedel	$^1/_{100}$	en hundradel

Ordinal numbers

First to twelfth:

1st	2nd	3rd	4th	5th	6th	7th	8th	9th	10th	11th	12th
1:a	2:a	3:e	4:e	5:e	6:e	7:e	8:e	9:e	10:e	11:e	12:e
första	andra	tredje	fjärde	femte	sjätte	sjunde	åttonde	nionde	tionde	elfte	tolfte

Thirteen to nineteen:
As cardinal numerals, but with the suffix **–de**.
Exampels: *trettonde* (13:e), *fjortonde* (14:e).

Even multiples of ten (20th to 90th):
As cardinal numerals, but with the suffix **–nde**.
Exampels: *tjugonde* (20:e), *trettionde* (30:e)

100th, 1000th:
As cardinal numerals, but with the suffix **–de**.
Examples: *hundrade* (100:e, hundredth), *tusende* (1000:e, thousandth)

Higher numbers:
As cardinal numerals, but with the suffix **-te**. There is no ordinal for "miljard" (billion).
Example: *miljonte* (millionth)

Exercises/Övningar!

Translate to Swedish (using only letters):

English	Swedish translation
2,634	
14,933	
Fivehundredfiftyfour	
It cost 12 kronor	
I'm 1.82 long. [1]	
The millionth visitor won a price.	

1) Note: In Sweden the metric system is used. 1.82 refers to 182 centimeters.

Translate to English:

Swedish	English translation
Femhundratusen är detsamma som en halv miljon.	
Tillsätt tre fjärdelar grädde.	
Åttatusentrehundrafyrtiofem	

Chapter 21 Answers

Translation to Swedish (using only letters):

English	Swedish translation
2,634	Tvåtusensexhundratrettiofyra
14,933	Fjortontusenniohundratrettiotre
Fivehundredfiftyfour	Femhundrafemtiofyra
It cost 12 kronor	Den kostar tolv kronor
I'm 1.82 long. [1]	Jag är en och åttiotvå (lång)
The millionth visitor won a price.	Den miljonte besökaren vann ett pris.

Translation to English:

Swedish	English translation
Femhundratusen är detsamma som en halv miljon.	Five hundred thousand is the same as half a million.
Tillsätt tre fjärdelar grädde.	Add three quarters of cream.
Åttatusentrehundrafyrtiofem	Eight Thousand Three Hundred Fortyfive (8,345)

Chapter 22: Verbs

Verbs do not inflect for person or number in modern standard Swedish. They inflect for the present tense, past tense, imperative, subjunctive, and indicative mood. Other tenses are formed by combinations of auxiliary verbs with infinitives or a special form of the participle called the "supine". In total there are 6 spoken active-voice forms for each verb: **infinitive, imperative, present, preterite/past, supine, and past participle**.

The only subjunctive form used in everyday speech is *vore*, the past subjunctive of *vara* ("to be"). It is used as one way of expressing the conditional ("would be", "were"), but is optional. Except for this form, subjunctive forms are considered archaic.

Verbs may also take the "passive voice". The passive voice for any verb tense is formed by appending *-s* to the tense. For verbs ending in *-r*, the *-r* is first removed before the *-s* is added. Verbs ending in *-er* often lose the *-e* as well, other than in very formal style: *stärker* (strengthens) becomes *stärks* or *stärkes* (is strengthened). (Exceptions are monosyllabic verbs and verbs where the root ends in *-s*.) Swedish uses the passive voice more frequently than English.

Conjugating verbs

Swedish verbs are divided into four groups:

Group	Description
1	regular *-ar* verbs
2	regular *-er* verbs
3	short verbs, end in *-r*
4	strong and irregular verbs, end in *-er* or *-r*

About 80% of all verbs in Swedish are group 1 verbs, which is the only productive verb group, i.e., all new verbs in Swedish are of this class. "Swenglish" variants of English verbs can be made by adding *-a* to the end of an English verb, sometimes with minor spelling changes. The verb is then treated as a group 1 verb. Examples of modern loan words within the IT field are **chatta** and **surfa**. Swenglish variants from the IT field that may be used but are not considered Swedish include **maila**, **mejla** (['mej̩la], to email or mail) and **savea**, **sejva** (['sej̩va] to save).

The stem of a verb is based on the present tense of the verb.
If the present tense ends in **-ar**, the **-r** is removed to form the stem, e.g., **kallar** → **kalla-**.
If the present tense ends in **-er**, the **-er** is removed, e.g., **stänger** → **stäng-**.
For short verbs, the **-r** is removed from the present tense of the verb, e.g., **syr** → **sy-**.
The imperative is the same as the stem.

For **group 1 verbs**, the stem ends in **-a**, the infinitive is the same as the stem, the present tense ends in **-r**, the past tense in **-de**, the supine in **-t**, and the past participle in **-d**, **-t**, and **de**.

For **group 2 verbs**, the stem ends in a **consonant**, the infinitive ends in **-a**, and the present tense in **-er**. Group 2 verbs are further subdivided into group 2a and 2b. For group 2a verbs, the past tense ends in **-de** and the past participle in **-d**, **-t**, and **-da**. For group 2b verbs, the past tense ends in **-te** and the past participle in **-t**, and **-ta**. This is in turn decided by whether the stem ends in a voiced or a voiceless consonant. E.g. the stem of **heta** (to be called) is **het**, and as **t** is a voiceless consonant the past tense ends in **-te**, making **hette** the past tense. If the stem ends in a voiced consonant however, as in **Stör-a** (to disturb), the past tense ends in **-de** making **störde** the past tense.

For **group 3 verbs**, the stem ends in a vowel that is <u>not</u> **-a**, the infinitive is the <u>same</u> as the stem, the present tense ends in **-r**, the past tense in **-dde**, the supine in **-tt**, and the past participle in **-dd**, **-tt**, and **-dda**.

Group 4 verbs are strong and irregular verbs. Many commonly used verbs belong to this group. For strong verbs, the vowel changes for the past and often the supine, following a definite pattern, e.g., **stryka** is a <u>strong verb</u> that follows the <u>u/y, ö, u pattern</u> (see table below for conjugations).
Irregular verbs, such as *vara* (to be), are completely irregular and follow no pattern. As of lately, an increasing number of verbs formerly conjugated with a strong inflection has been subject to be conjugated with its weak equivalent form in colloquial speech.

Group	Stem	Imper	Infinitive	Present	Preterite/	Supine	Past	Englis

	-ative					Past				participle		h
1	*kalla-*	*kalla!*	*kalla*	-	*kallar*	-r	*kallade*	-de	*kallat*	-t	*kallad* -d *kallat* -t *kallade* -de	to call
2a	*stäng-*	*stäng!*	*stänga*	-a	*stänger*	-er	*stängde*	-de	*stängt*	-t	*stängd* -d *stängt* -t *stängda* -da	to close
2b	*läs-*	*läs!*	*läsa*	-a	*läser*	-er	*läste*	-te	*läst*	-t	*läst* -t *läst* -t *lästa* -ta	to read
3	*sy-*	*sy!*	*sy*	-	*syr*	-r	*sydde*	-dde	*sytt*	-tt	*sydd* -dd *sytt* -tt *sydda* -dda	to sew
4, strong	*stryk-*	*stryk!*	*stryka*	-a	*stryker*	-er	*strök*	*	*strukit*	-it	*struken* -en *struket* -et *strukna* -na	to strike-out to iron to stroke
4, irregular	*var-*	*var!*	*vara*		*är*		*var*		*varit*		-	to be

*often new vowel

Examples of tenses with English translations

Tense	English	Swedish
Infinitiv	To work	*(Att) arbet**a***
Present Tense	I work	*Jag arbeta**r***
Past Tense, Imperfect Aspekt	I worked	*Jag arbeta**de***
Past Tense, Perfect Aspekt	*I have worked*	Jag har arbeta**t**
Future Tense, Futurum Simplex	*I will work*	*Jag ska arbeta*

The irregular verb *gå*

Tense	English	Swedish

Infinitiv	To walk	*(Att) gå*
Present Tense	I walk	*Jag går*
Past Tense, Imperfect Aspekt	I walked	*Jag gick*
Past Tense, Perfect Aspekt	I have walked	*Jag har gått*
Future Tense, Futurum Simplex	I will walk	*Jag ska gå*

As in all the Germanic languages, strong verbs change their vowel sounds in the various tenses. For most Swedish strong verbs that have a verb cognate in English or German, that cognate is also strong. For example, "to bite" is a strong verb in all three languages:

Language	Infinitive	Present	Preterite/Past	Supine/Perfect	Past participle
Swedish	*bita*	*jag biter*	*jag bet*	*jag har bitit*	*biten, bitet, bitna*
Dutch	*bijten*	*ik bijt*	*ik beet*	*ik heb gebeten*	*gebeten*
German	*beißen*	*ich beiße*	*ich biss*	*ich habe gebissen*	*gebissen*
English	to bite	I bite	I bit	I have bitten	bitten

Supine form

The supine (supinum) form is used in Swedish to form the composite past form of a verb. For verb groups 1-3 the supine is identical to the neuter form of the past participle. For verb group 4, the supine ends in *-it* while the past participle's neuter form ends in *-et*.

This is best shown by example:

Simple past:	I ate (the) dinner	*Jag åt maten* (using preterite)
Composite past:	I have eaten (the) dinner	*Jag har **ätit** maten* (using supine)
Past participle common:	(The) dinner is eaten	*Maten är **äten*** (using past participle)
Past participle neuter:	(The) apple is eaten	*Äpplet är **ätet***
Past participle plural:	(The) apples are eaten	*Äpplena är **ätna***

The supine form is used after **ha** (to have). In English this form is normally merged with the past participle, or the preterite, and this was formerly the case in Swedish, too (the choice of *-it* or *-et* being dialectal rather than grammatical); however, in modern Swedish, they are separate, since the distinction of *-it* being supine and *-et* being participial was standardised.

Passive voice

The passive voice in Swedish is formed in one of four ways:
1. add an *-s* to the infinitive form of the verb
2. use a form of **bli** (become) + the perfect participle
3. use a form of **vara** (be) + the perfect participle
4. use a form of **få** (get) + the perfect participle

Of the first three forms, the first (**s**-passive) tends to focus on the action itself rather than the result of it. The second (**bli**-passive) stresses the change caused by the action. The third (**vara**-passive) puts the result of the action in the centre of interest:

1. *Dörren målas.* (Someone paints the door right now.)

2. *Dörren blir målad.* (The door is being painted, in a new colour or wasn't painted before.)

3. *Dörren är målad.* (The door is painted.)

The fourth form is different from the others, since it is analogous to the English "get-passive": *Han fick dörren målad* (He got the/his door painted). This form is used when you want to use a subject other than the "normal" one in a passive clause. In English you could say: "The door was painted for him", but if you want "he" to be the subject you need to say "He got the door painted." Swedish uses the same structure.

The subjunctive mood

Verbs in the subjunctive mood, in Swedish termed *Konjunktiv*, are conjugated in two tenses - Present and Past. Present subjunctive forms are rarely heard in modern Swedish. Their use is restricted to frozen expressions like *Leve kungen!*, Long live the king!, and *Följe lyckan dig genom livet!*, Let luck follow you in this life!. Present subjunctive is formed by adding the "-e" ending to the stem of a verb:

Infinitive	Indicative	Subjunctive (very, very unusual)
att tala, to speak	*talar*, speak(s)	*tale*, may speak
att bliva, to become	*bli(ve)r*, become(s)	*blive*, may become
att skriva, to write	*skriver*, write(s)	*skrive*, may write
att springa, to run	*springer*, run(s)	*springe*, may run

Past subjunctive forms are more frequent than Present ones, although becoming increasingly rare in speech as well as in texts in Standard Swedish. Past subjunctive is however still regularly used in certain country dialects. For weak verbs the Subjunctive Past is indistinguishable from Indicative Past, but for strong verbs, the Subjunctive irregularly attains either the Preterite form adding an *-e* suffix, or the Supine form, replacing *-it* with *-e*:

Infinitive	Indicative	Subjunctive (very, very unusual)
att tala, to speak	*talade*, spoke	*talade*, (may) have spoken
att bli(va), to become	*blev*, became	*bleve*, (may) have become
att skriva, to write	*skrev*, wrote	*skreve*, (may) have written
att springa, to run	*sprang*, ran	*sprunge*, (may) have run

Exercises/Övningar!

Translate to Swedish with the verbs in the correct form:

English	Swedish translation
He <u>travels</u> to Chile tomorrow.	
I <u>ate</u> a lot of salad.	
Can you <u>read</u> this?	
She <u>lived</u> in New York.	
I have never <u>spoken</u> Swedish.	

We <u>went</u> skiing in the Andes.	
I <u>closed</u> the door, can you <u>close</u> the windows?	
Did you <u>call</u> on me?	
I have <u>walked</u> all the way.	
I'm <u>going to</u> live in Malmö?	
I <u>ate</u> mine, have you <u>eaten</u> yours?	
Will you hit me since I hit you?	

Put the irregular word *springa* (run) in its correct form:

Tense	English	Swedish
Infinitiv	To run	
Present Tense	I run	
Past Tense, Imperfect Aspekt	I ran	
Past Tense, Perfect Aspekt	I have run	
Future Tense, Futurum Simplex	I will run	

Chapter 22 Answers

Translation to Swedish:

English	Swedish translation
He <u>travels</u> to Chile tomorrow.	Han reser till Chile imorgon.
I <u>ate</u> a lot of salad.	Jag <u>åt</u> en massa sallad.
Can you <u>read</u> this?	Kan du <u>läsa</u> detta?
She <u>lived</u> in New York.	Hon <u>bodde</u> i New York.
I have never <u>spoken</u> Swedish.	Jag har aldrig <u>pratat</u> svenska.
We <u>went</u> skiing in the Andes.	Vi <u>åkte</u> skidor I Anderna.
I <u>closed</u> the door, can you <u>close</u> the windows?	Jag <u>stängde</u> dörren, kan du **stänga** fönstren?
Did you <u>call</u> on me?	<u>Kallade</u> du på mig?
I have <u>walked</u> all the way.	Jag har <u>gått</u> hela vägen.
I'm <u>going to</u> live in Malmö?	Jag <u>kommer att</u> bo i Malmö.
I <u>ate</u> mine, have you <u>eaten</u> yours?	Jag <u>åt</u> min, har du <u>ätit</u> din?
Will you hit me since I hit you?	Kommer du slå mig eftersom jag slog dig?

The irregular word *springa* (run) in its correct form:

Tense	English	Swedish
Infinitiv	To run	*(Att) springa*
Present Tense	I run	*Jag springer*
Past Tense, Imperfect Aspekt	I ran	*Jag sprang*
Past Tense, Perfect Aspekt	I have run	*Jag har sprungit*
Future Tense, Futurum Simplex	I will run	*Jag ska springa*

Chapter 23: Adverbs

Adjectival adverbs are formed by putting the adjective in neuter singular form. Adjectives ending in *-lig* may take either the neuter singular ending or the suffix *-en*, and occasionally *-ligen* is added to an adjective not already ending in *-lig*.

Common	Neuter	Adverb
tjock, thick	*tjockt*, thick	*tjockt*, thickly
snabb, fast	*snabbt*, fast	*snabbt*, fast
avsiktlig, intentional	*avsiktligt*, intentional	*avsiktligt, avsiktligen*, intentionally
stor, great, large	*stort*, great, large	*storligen*, greatly *i stort sett*, largely

Directional adverbs

Adverbs of direction in Swedish show a distinction that is lacking in English: some have different forms exist depending on whether one is heading that way, or already there.

Example: *Jag steg **upp** på taket. Jag arbetade där **uppe** på taket.*
            (I climbed **up** on the roof. I was working **up** there on the roof).

Heading that way	Already there	English
upp	*uppe*	up
ner	*nere*	down
in	*inne*	in
ut	*ute*	out
hem	*hemma*	home
bort	*borta*	away
fram	*framme*	forward

Exercises/Övningar!

Translate to Swedish:

English	Swedish translation
I am <u>down</u> here but want <u>up</u> so I can sit with you <u>up</u> there and look <u>down</u>.	
I'm going <u>away</u> because I don't want to be at <u>home</u>.	
When I'm <u>in</u> I can look <u>out</u> the window.	

Chapter 23 Answers

Translation to Swedish:

English	Swedish translation
I am <u>down</u> here but want <u>up</u> so I can sit with you <u>up</u> there and look <u>down</u>.	Jag är här <u>nere</u> men vill <u>upp</u> så jag kan sitta med dig där <u>uppe</u> och titta <u>ner</u>.
I'm going <u>away</u> because I don't want to be at <u>home</u>.	Jag ska åka <u>bort</u> för jag vill inte vara <u>hemma</u>.
When I'm <u>in</u> I can look <u>out</u> the window.	När jag är <u>inne</u> kan jag se <u>ut</u> genom fönstret.

Chapter 24: Prepositions

Unlike in more conservative Germanic languages (e.g. German), putting a noun into a prepositional phrase doesn't alter its inflection, case, number or definiteness in any way.

Prepositions of location

Preposition	Meaning	Example	Translation
på	on	Råttan dansar **på** bordet.	The rat dances on the table.
under	under	Musen dansar **under** bordet.	The mouse dances under the table.
i	in	Kålle arbetar **i** Göteborg.	Kålle works in Gothenburg.
till	to	Ada har åkt **till** Göteborg.	Ada has gone to Gothenburg.

Prepositions of time

Preposition	Meaning	Example	Translation
på	at	Vi ses **på** rasten.	See you at the break.
före	before	De var alltid trötta **före** rasten.	They were always tired before the break.
om	in	Kan vi ha rast **om** en timme?	May we have a break in one hour?
i	for	Kan vi ha rast **i** en timme?	May we have a break for one hour?
på	for (in a negative statement)	Vi har inte haft rast **på** två timmar.	We have not had a break for two hours.

under	during	Vi arbetade **under** helgdagarna.	We worked during the holidays.

Casual prepositions

Preposition	Meaning	Example	Translation
över	about	Kålle är glad **över** att ha träffat Ada.	Kålle is happy about having met Ada.
med	with	Kålle är nöjd **med** Ada.	Kålle is pleased with Ada.
på	of	Kålle är trött **på** Ada.	Kålle is tired of Ada.
av	from	Kålle är trött **av** nattskiftet.	Kålle is tired from the nightshift. (because of the nightshift)

Placement of prepositions

Often prepositions are placed before the word they are referring to. However, there are a few exceptions:

Preposition	Meaning	Example	Translation
runt	around	riket **runt**	around the Kingdom
emellan	between	bröder **emellan**	between brothers

Exercises/Övningar!

Translate to Swedish:

English	Swedish translation
Eva lives in Stockholm but she often travels to Gothenburg.	
I live on the third floor and you live in the apartment just under me.	
I havn't eaten for six hours.	
Wash your hands before you eat.	
I was sick during my vacation.	
I see you at the restaurant.	

I am tired of you.	
I am so disappointed about having to quit.	
The boat circled around the island.	

Chapter 24 Answers

Translation to Swedish:

English	Swedish translation
Eva lives in Stockholm but she often travels to Gothenburg.	Eva bor i Stockholm men hon reser ofta till Göteborg.
I live on the third floor and you live in the apartment just under me.	Jag bor på tredje våningen och du bor i våningen precis under mig.
I havn't eaten for six hours.	Jag har inte ätit på sex timmar.
Wash your hands before you eat.	Tvätta händerna före du äter.
I was sick during my vacation.	Jag var sjuk under min semester.
I see you at the restaurant.	Vi ses på restaurangen.
I am tired of you.	Jag är trött på dig.
I am so disappointed about having to quit.	Jag är så besviken över att behöva sluta.
The boat circled around the island.	Båten cirklade runt ön.

Conclusion

Now, Embark on Your Own Adventure!

Now you are ready to go out there and start communicating in the basic Swedish that you have learned from this book. Keep in mind that you have not learned how to say *everything* in Swedish, but you are equipped to make a great start and work your way around using what you now know. Don't forget the basic language skills that you have learned in this book. If you don't know how to say something, ask, use context clues, describe it using the language that you know, and you will eventually find the answer.

Don't worry about looking silly and just do your best to learn from the mistakes you make! Keep a journal to write about your experiences and the new things that you are learning every day. Though it's not always easy and sometimes rather frustrating, traveling abroad is one of the most rewarding experiences you will have. I hope this book has prepared you well and wish you many exciting and fulfilling adventures in your travels!

To your success,

Dagny Taggart

PS: Can I Ask You a Quick Favor?

If you liked the book please leave a nice review on Amazon! I'd absolutely love to hear your feedback. Please go to Amazon right now (following the link below), and write down a quick line sharing with me your experience. I personally read ALL the reviews there, and I'm thrilled to hear your feedback and honest motivation. It's what keeps me going, and helps me improve everyday =)

Go to Amazon by following this link and write a quick review!

>> http://www.amazon.com/Swedish-Ultimate-Learning-Language-Portuguese-ebook/dp/B00PE72NYU/ <<

***
ONCE YOU'RE BACK,
FLIP THE PAGE!
BONUS CHAPTER AHEAD
=)

Learn Any Language 300% FASTER

>> Get Full Online Language Courses With Audio Lessons <<

Would you like to learn a new language? I think that's a great idea. Now, why don't you do it 300% *FASTER*?

I've partnered with the most revolutionary language teachers to bring you the very language online courses I've ever seen. It's a mind-blowing program specifically created for language hackers such as ourselves. It will allow you learn ANY language, from French to Chinese, 3x faster, straight from the comfort of your own home, office, or wherever you may be. It's like having an unfair advantage!

You can choose from a wide variety of languages, such as French, Spanish, Italian, German, Chinese, Portuguese, and A TON more.

Each Online Course consists of:

+ 91 Built-In Lessons
+ 33 Interactive Audio Lessons
+ 24/7 Support to Keep You Going

The program is extremely engaging, fun, and easy-going. You won't even notice you are learning a complex foreign language from scratch. And before you realize it, by the time you go through all the lessons you will officially become a truly solid speaker.

Old classrooms are a thing of the past. It's time for a revolution.

If you'd like to go the extra mile, the click the button below or follow the link, and let the revolution begin

>> http://www.bitly.com/Foreign-Languages <<

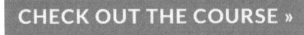

CHECK OUT THE COURSE »

Preview Of "Learn French In 7 DAYS! - The Ultimate Crash Course on Learning The Basics of the French Language In No Time"

Introduction

Why should YOU learn French?

Backpacking in the South of France? Dating a dreamy French man or a beautiful French lady? Planning a business meeting with French clients? Moving to a French-speaking country? Willing to show off at the next French festival of your local town?...

This book is for ALL OF YOU!

Thanks to this book, you'll get a grasp of what is French and how to master it! This book will offer you a complete overview of the language along with useful expressions to start speaking.

French is a difficult language to learn... that's why this book makes it fun and easy... without forgetting efficiency!

By the end of this course, you will get the amazing feeling that YOU CAN DO IT! YOU CAN SPEAK FRENCH!

How will YOU learn French within a few weeks?

Are you aware that as an English speaker, you already know some 15,000 French words. The English language has indeed been shaped by many other languages, such as Latin, German, French.

The French influence on English dates back to the Norman invasion of England in 1066. It had a major impact not only on the country but on the language itself. William the Conqueror brought Norman French which became the language of the court, the government and the upper class for the next three centuries. During the Norman occupation, around 10,000 French words were adopted into English, of which about 75% are still used today. More than 30% of all English words are derived directly or indirectly from French.

If that doesn't convince you to learn French, the idea of visiting one of the 33 French-speaking countries over the world might do it!

French and English are the only languages spoken as a native language on 5 continents and the only languages taught in every country in the world. French is the official or one of the official languages in 33 countries[1]. This number is second to English, which is officially spoken in 45 countries.

Let's not wait anymore and indulge yourself in our learning program... and most of all, ENJOY every bit of the journey!

Chapter 1 : Introducing French

What you're about to learn:

→ How to use French words you already know
→ How to be at ease with French pronounciation

French/English similarities

The Normans brought French into the English language which resulted in more than 30% of French words currently being used by English natives. You may not be aware of it but everyday... you speak French!

Many of the words of French origin used in English find their roots in Latin and/or Greek. As an example, "beef" from French "boeuf" is meat from a cow (from old English "cu") which is a type of "bovine" from Latin "bovinus" via French "bovin".

---

1   French is the official language of France and its overseas territories (French Guyana, Guadeloupe, Martinique, Mayotte, La Réunion, French Polynesia, New Caledonia, Saint Barts, Saint Martin, Saint Pierre and Miquelon, Wallis and Futuna) as well as 14 other countries: Bénin, Burkina Faso, Central African Republic, Democratic Republic of Congo, Republic of Congo, Côte d'Ivoire, Gabon, Guinea, Luxembourg, Mali, Monaco, Niger, Sénégal, Togo.

French is also one of the official languages in the following countries: Belgium, Burundi, Cameroon, Canada, Chad, Channel Islands (Guernsey and Jersey), Comoros, Djibouti, Equatorial, Guinea, Haiti (the other official language is French Creole), Madagascar, Rwanda, Seychelles, Switzerland, Vanuatu.

For a clearer comprehension of the similarities, we have divided this paragraph into four different aspects related to the French influence in English language. There are original French words and expressions to be found in English, true cognates ("vrais amis"), false cognates ("faux amis") and spelling equivalents.

This will make it easier to understand how to use French words you already know and use in English!

French words & expressions in English

Over the years, an important number of French words and expressions have been absorbed by the English language and are still intact. Many English speakers might not even realize that they are using these French words in everyday conversations.
Some other words and expressions have been kept to add *a certain touch of French* – "un certain je ne sais quoi". English speakers seem to be aware of this French influence and intentionally using those words with a somewhat accurate pronunciation!

Below is a list of some common examples of French words and expressions used in English.

"adieu" : farewell
"à la carte" : on the menu
"à la mode" : in fashion/style (in English "with ice-cream")
"art déco" : decorative art
"au pair" : a person who works for a family in exchange for room and board
"avant-garde" : innovative (arts)
"brunette" : small, dark-haired female
"cordon bleu" : master chef
"coup d'état" : government overthrow
"cuisine" : type of food/cooking
"débutante" : beginner (In French, "débutante" is the feminine form of "débutant" which means in English beginner (noun) or beginning (adj). In both languages, it refers to a young girl making her formal début into society. Interestingly this usage is not original in French. It was adopted back from English.)
"déjà-vu" : feeling like you've already seen or done something
"haute couture" : high-class clothing style
"Mardi Gras" : Shrove Tuesday
"pot-pourri" : cented mixture of dried flowers and spices

"prêt-à-porter" : clothing
"savoir-faire" : know-how
"savoir-vivre" : manners, etiquette
"souvenir" : memento
"Bon appétit!" : Enjoy your meal!
"Bon voyage!" : Have a good trip!
"C'est la vie!" : That's life!
"Oh là là!" : Ooh la la!
"RSVP" ("Répondez s'il vous plaît") : Please RSVP
"Touché!" : You got me!
"Voilà!" : There it is!

True cognates ("vrais amis")

True cognates (true friends) are words with identical spelling and meaning in both French and English. Given the great use of these words in English, you already have a considerable asset to start using French vocabulary!

True cognates are pronounced differently most of the time. However the exact spelling makes it a great advantage to learn French as an English speaker. You can easily learn some French phrases that have several true cognates.

For instance, "je vais voir un film au cinéma ce week-end avec mon cousin" can be understood with the words "film", "cinema", "weekend" and "cousin". You can easily come up with a translation thanks to the French cognates: "I will go to the movies this weekend with my cousin".

Note: "cousin" is used in both French and English to refer to the son (or daughter in English) of one of your sibling. While it remains the same for male and female in English, the feminine form has a different spelling in French: "cousine".

Did you really think that it was so hard to speak French? Just start using the hundreds of words you already use everyday!
The list of French cognates is incredibly long – they are estimated to be some 1,700 words! The following list is just a sample of some of the most common true cognates used in English.

Useful to learn French:

"accent" (masculine noun)
"alphabet" (masculine)

Useful words at work:

"absence" (feminine noun)
"accident" (masculine)
"client" (masculine)
"collaboration" (feminine)
"communication" (feminine)
"contact" (masculine)
"document" (masculine)
"fax" (masculine)
"message" (masculine)
"mission" (feminine)
"obligation" (feminine)
"payable" (adjective)
"profession" (feminine)
"solution" (feminine)
"test" (masculine)

Planning your weekend get-away:

"barbecue" (masculine)
"bikini" (masculine)
"bistro" (masculine)
"bungalow" (masculine)
"camp" (masculine)
"casino" (masculine)
"concert" (masculine)
"kayak" (masculine noun)
"parachute" (masculine)
"parasol" (masculine)
"promenade" (feminine)
"ski" (masculine)
"sport" (masculine)
"taxi" (masculine)
"tennis" (masculine)
"valise" (feminine)
"zoo" (masculine)

At the restaurant:

"addition" (feminine)
"apéritif" (masculine)
"chef" (masculine)
"dessert" (masculine)
"entrée" (feminine)
"fruit" (masculine)
"gourmet" (masculine)
"hors-d'oeuvre" (masculine)
"menu" (masculine)
"pizza" (feminine)
"quiche" (feminine)
"sorbet" (masculine)
"steak" (masculine)
"vodka" (feminine)

False cognates ("faux-amis")

In French, there are numerous "faux-amis" (false cognates or false friends). These words can cause communication problems as they look alike in French and English but have a totally different meaning.

A wrong use of a false friend can end up by a funny joke or a lack of respect. As an example, it can be funny to hear that someone never buys food containing "préservatifs", which in French means "condoms"! However it would not be clever to mistake "pain", which means "bread" in French, with the actual English word (the correct French word being "douleur"). You never know what you will end up getting at the drugstore!

Here is a list of the most common "faux-amis" to avoid stupid mistakes that will haunt you forever!

French faux ami	English translation
actuel	Current, present
actuellement	Currently, presently
agenda	diary
allure	pace, appearance, style
assister à	to attend

attendre	to wait
avertissement	warning
balance	scale
blesser	to wound
bribes	fragments
car	coach
cave	cellar
chair	flesh
chance	luck
coin	corner
déception	disappointment
demander	to ask for
éventuellement	possibly
fabrique	factory
formidable	terrific
génial	brilliant
gentil	kind
injures	insult
lecture	reading
nouvelle	piece of news, short story
patron	boss
préservatif	condom
procès	trial
prune	plum
quitter	to leave
rester	to stay
sensible	sensitive
tissu	fabric

The use of "Franglais"

"Franglais" refers to the massive invasion of French by English words and expressions thanks to the globalization, bringing a worldwide popular culture, and the access to the internet. It has become trendy to use English words in French language. Despite many efforts, the French have failed into translating these English words in their own language, unlike the Canadian French who remarkably succeed in finding equivalents for every English word!

Below is a short list of the most common English words used by French speakers:

baby-foot	table football
basket	Sports shoe, basketball
brushing	blow-dry
camping	campsite
dressing	walk-in closet
catch	wrestling
flipper	pinball machine
footing	jogging
forcing	pressure
jogging	tracksuit
lifting	face-lift
people	celebrity
planning	schedule
pressing	dry-cleaner
relooking	make-over
smoking	tuxedo
sweat	sweatshirt
warning	hazard lights

Pronunciation

The French alphabet has the same number of letters as the English one. There are 6 vowels ("une voyelle") and 20 consonants ("une consonne").

A **vowel** is a sound that is pronounced through the mouth (or the nose for nasal vowels) with no obstruction of the lips, tongue, or throat.
There are a few general guidelines to keep in mind when pronouncing French vowels:
➔Most French vowels are pronounced further forward in the mouth than their English counterparts.

➔The tongue must remain tensed throughout the pronunciation of the vowel.

As for the **consonants**, many of them are similar in French and English so they should be quite easy to learn.

As an approach to French pronunciation ("la prononciation"), we propose you to use the following guide throughout the chapters.

Always refer to this pronunciation guide whenever you try to say a French word from our book. You can also complement your studies with vocal guides to be easily found on the Internet.

Simple letters **("les lettres simples"):**

French letters	Sounds like	English examples	French examples
a	a	r[a]t	bras (arm), chat (cat)
b	b	[b]utter	bateau (boat), bébé (baby)
c before o,a,u	k	[c]andy	carte (map), col (collar)
c before e,i,y	s	[s]tanza	citron (lemon), ciment (cement)
ç	s	[s]ilence	ça (this), garçon (boy)
d	d	[d]og	dos (back), dans (in)
e	u	b[u]bble	le (the), ce (this)
f	f	[f]ood	faire (to make), fleur (flower)
g before o,a,u	g	[g]row	gauche (left), guerre (war)
g before e,i,y	j	dé[j]à vu	orange (orange), girafe (giraffe)
h always silent	–	–	hibou (owl), hache (ax)
i	ee	f[ee]t	bisou (kiss), cri (shout)
j	j	dé[j]à vu	je (I), jamais (never)

k	k	[k]oala	képi (kepi), koala (koala)
l	l	[l]ove	lapin (rabbit), livre (book)
m	m	[m]other	maman (mom), mon (mine)
n	n	[n]ever	non (no), nid (nest)
o	o	z[o]rro	domino (domino), collègue (colleague)
p	p	[p]asta	papa (dad), patate (potatoe)
q	q	[c]ap	quatre (four), qui (who)
r	r	a[r]t deco	rare (unsual), radis (radish)
s	s	[s]nail	son (sound), savoir (know)
t	t	[t]ag	tata (auntie), ton (your)
u	ew	déjà v[u]	tu (you), ruban (ribbon)
v	v	[v]iew	vivre (to live), venir (to come)
w	v	wa[v]e	wagon
w (English origin)	w	[w]ater	whisky, wapiti
x inside a word or when ex- is followed by a consonnant or at the end of words	x	e[x]cess	expert, luxe (luxury)
x at the begining of a word or when ex- is followed by a vowel or h	x	e[x]am	exemple (example), examen (exam, test)
x at the end of words	s	[s]olution	dix (ten), six (six)
x (rare cases)	z	[z]ero	deuxième (second)
x at the end of words to indicate	silent	–	choux (cabbages), chevaux (horses)

plural			
y	y	[y]am	yoyo, yacht
z	z	[z]ip	zéro (zero), zèbre (zebra)

Complex sounds ("les sons complexes"):

French sounds	Sounds like	English examples	French examples
ai	ai	l[ai]ssez-faire	aimer (to love), faire (to do)
-ain, -aim	un	Verd[un]	pain (bread), faim (hunger)
au	o	r[o]pe	paume (palm), baume (balm)
ch	sh	[sh]ampoo	château (castle), chapeau (hat)
ei	e	m[e]n	peine (pain), reine (queen)
eu	e	th[e]	peu (little), deux (two)
-er, -ez	a	d[a]y	manger (to eat), vous allez (you go)
eau, -aud, -ot	o	[o]zone	rateau (rake), chaud (hot), pot (jar)
em, en before consonant	en	[en]core	entre (between), emploi (job)
ha-	a	r[a]t	habiter (to live)
ill	y	[y]ogurt	fille (girl), billet (ticket)
oi	wa	[wa]ter	toit (roof), quoi (what)
oin	oo + un	t[oo]+Verd[un]	loin (far), coin (corner)
on, om	on	s[on]g	bon (good), chanson (song)
ou	oo	t[wo]	fou (crazy), cou (neck)

ph	f	[f]ather	phare (lighthouse)
sc before o,a,u	sc	[sc]oundrel	sculpter (to sculpt), scorpion
sc before e,i,y	sc	[sc]enario	scie (saw), scène (stage)
th	t	[t]ime	thym (thyme), thèse (thesis)
ti	s	[s]tone	objection (objection), prophétie (prophecy)
um, un word ending or before a consonant	un	Verd[un]	un (a), parfum (perfume)
ui	wi	ki[wi]	pluie (rain), cuisine (kitchen)

Accents ("les accents")

French letters	Sounds like	English examples	French examples
à	a	r[a]t	à (in)
é	a	d[a]y	école (school), café (coffee)
è, ê	e	m[e]n	père (father), mère (mother)
â,î,ô,û pronounced as a,i,o,u			château (castle), hôpital (hospital) …
ä, ë, ï, ö, ü the tréma indicates that the two adjacent vowels must both be pronounced	a i	n[a i]ve	Noël (Christmas), haïr (to hate)

"Test your French!"

Let's review what you've learnt in that chapter with a few exercises.

Mark the correct answers:

In French, "people" is used to mean:
□ a young person
□ an old person
□ a celebrity

In English, "brilliant" is the translation of the following French word:
□ brilliant
□ épatant
□ génial

In French, "brunette" refers to :
□ a type of food
□ a small, dark-haired female
□ a painting color

Which of the following words is a true cognate (true friend)?"
□ actually
□ car
□ pot-pourri

Which of the following is a false cognate (false friend)?
□ préservatif
□ débutante
□ gourmet

Which of the following English term uses the French sound "eau" like in "chapeau" (hat)?
□ face
□ throw
□ shampoo

Which of the following English term uses the French sound "ai" like in "aimer" (to love)?
□ well
□ parade
□ three

Answers:

In French, "people" is used to mean:
☐ a celebrity

In English, "brilliant" is the translation of the following French word:
☐ génial

In French, "brunette" refers to :
☐ a small, dark-haired female

Which of the following words is a true cognate (true friend)?"
☐ pot-pourri

Which of the following is a false cognate (false friend)?
☐ préservatif

Which of the following English term uses the French sound "eau" like in "chapeau" (hat)?
☐ throw

Which of the following English term uses the French sound "ai" like in "aimer" (to love)?
☐ well

Click here to check out the rest of "Learn French In 7 DAYS! - The Ultimate Crash Course on Learning The Basics of the French Language In No Time" on Amazon

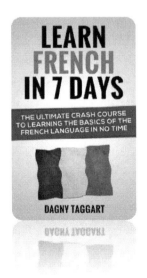

Ps: You'll find many more books like these under my name, Dagny Taggart. Don't miss them! Here's a short list:

- Learn **Spanish** In 7 Days!
- Learn **French** In 7 Days!
- Learn **German** In 7 Days!
- Learn **Italian** In 7 Days!
- Learn **Portuguese** In 7 Days!

- Learn **Japanese** In 7 Days!
- Learn **Chinese** In 7 Days!

- Learn **Russian** In 7 Days!

- Learn Any Language FAST!

- How to Drop Everything & Travel Around The World

Check Out My Other Books

Are you ready to exceed your limits? Then pick a book from the one below and start learning yet another new language. I can't imagine anything more fun, fulfilling, and exciting!

If you'd like to see the entire list of language guides (there are a ton more!), go to:

>>http://www.amazon.com/Dagny-Taggart/e/B00K54K6CS/<<

About the Author

Dagny Taggart is a language enthusiast and polyglot who travels the world, inevitably picking up more and more languages along the way.

 Taggart's true passion became learning languages after she realized the incredible connections with people that it fostered. Now she just can't get enough of it. Although it's taken time, she has acquired vast knowledge on the best and fastest ways to learn languages. But the truth is, she is driven simply by her motive to build exceptional links and bonds with others.

She is inspired everyday by the individuals she meets across the globe. For her, there's simply not anything as rewarding as practicing languages with others because she gets to make friends with people from all that come from a variety of cultures. This, in turn, has broadened her mind and thinking more than she would have ever imagined it could.

Of course, as a result of her constant travels, Taggart has become an expert on planning trips and making the most of time spent out of what she calls her "base" town. She jokes that she's practically at the nomad status now, but she's more content to live that way.

She knows how to live on a manageable budget weather she's in Paris or Phnom Penh. She knows how to seek out the adventures and thrills, no doubt, lying in wait at any city she visits. She knows that reflection on each every experience is significant if she wants to grow as a traveler and student of the world's cultures.

Because of this, Taggart chooses to share her understanding of languages and travel so that others, too, can experience the same life-altering benefits she has.

Printed in Great Britain
by Amazon.co.uk, Ltd.,
Marston Gate.